Where to Legally Invest, Live & Work Without Paying any Taxes

by
Adam Starchild

International Law and Taxation Publishers

London

Where to Legally Invest, Live & Work Without Paying any Taxes

by
Adam Starchild

ISBN 1-893713-13-X

International Law & Taxation Publishers
London
http://www.internationallawandtaxationpublishers.com

Contents

Introduction

Like most people, you are probably paying too much in taxes. Even if you have taken measures to reduce your tax burden, you are still likely paying too much. The typical tax hedges and plans designed to reduce taxes are largely inadequate, hardly reducing taxes to any significant degree.

Unquestionably, taxes are one of the biggest hindrances to an individual's efforts to provide for his or her family. The more you pay in taxes, the less you have to buy your family the things they need and enjoy. Reduce your taxes by $5,000 per year and you may take an extra vacation, you may invest it to later help pay for a child's education, or you may invest it to earn more money, in time building a sizable portfolio. Of course, you may simply spend the money any way you like. After all, it is your money.

There is an old saying: "The only two things you can count on in life are death and taxes." That may have been true in the past, but there are opportunities that can substantially reduce your tax burden, and, in some cases, relieve you of it entirely.

Several countries and jurisdictions throughout the world offer impressive incentives and plans through which you can greatly minimize your tax burden. Some have passed legislation that supports a business friendly environment — providing a host of tax advantages, a minimization of red tape, and a variety of grants and special plans that are designed to increase a company's edge in an increasingly competitive economic climate. Other places offer various tax incentives to individuals. Indeed, there are places where you can live virtually tax-free. In the following pages, the most advantageous of these countries and jurisdictions will be examined. These are by no means backwater enclaves or small municipalities; they are highly desirable places to live, work, and invest. Some prefer to remain reticent about the financial benefits they offer, while others openly promote their tax and investment plans and incentives. If you genuinely desire to reduce your tax burden, all deserve careful consideration.

All of these countries and jurisdictions are collectively referred to as *tax havens.* In its simplest definition, a tax haven is a place that enacts legislation designed to decrease the tax burden on investors. The typical tax haven seeks to attract investors from around the world.

You might be wondering why a place would offer tax benefits to both its citizens and foreigners. By offering major tax incentives to investors, tax haven countries and jurisdictions increase the amount of money that flows into the tax haven. This money can then be used to stimulate the tax haven's economy. The underlying principal here is that low taxes result in economic growth.

To take full advantage of some of these opportunities, you may need to satisfy residency requirements. Some countries require that you remain in the country for a particular length of time to benefit from tax incentives; others have few or negligible conditions that you must meet. In some, to fully take advantage of their tax laws, you must become a citizen. This is often not as daunting as it sounds, because in most cases, you will be able to carry dual citizenship. Thus, if you are a citizen of the United States, you may also become a citizen of another nation. Of course, this can become tricky under some circumstances, and you should always research your situation carefully, assessing your plans and goals in the light of each country's laws. For some people, it is quite beneficial to change their citizenship if it results in major tax savings.

Some words of caution are necessary here:

- If you are thinking of moving to another country to take advantage of its tax laws, be sure that you carefully consider the country's geography, climate, people, history, and government. Will you enjoy living there? Do you find the physical surroundings pleasant? Do you like the people, the country's traditions and customs? Are you comfortable with its language and social practices? Are you satisfied with the way companies conduct their business? Are there enjoyable recreational activities available to you? Will you be able to settle into a comfortable lifestyle? Will you feel secure in this new land? Will you have access to the kinds of conveniences you are accustomed to? Does the country have a quality system of health care? In short, after answering the questions above, and similar questions, are you sure that you will be happy there? Only consider moving to another country if the answer is an unhesitating yes.

- Whenever you are considering committing money to any investment plan or company, always investigate the plan or company thoroughly. Carefully assess the incentives it offers, as well as any potential drawbacks.

Carefully weigh any risks against possible benefits. Consider the following types of questions. What is the past record? Has the company or plan shown steady profits? Are they stable? How experienced is management? Are there any external regional, domestic, or international factors that might positively or negatively affect either the plan or company? What are the likely short-term and long-term prospects?

- Find out as much about the country or jurisdiction as you can. Write to the country's embassy for information. Note that many tax havens maintain special agencies that provide information and various services to investors. Contact them and obtain as much information as you can. Once you receive any information, review it carefully, with a critical eye. You should then weigh the information you have obtained with information from other sources. News magazines and international business magazines usually contain excellent in-depth information about countries and regions of the world.

- If you are planning to make a sizable investment, it would be wise to visit the country or jurisdiction you are considering. This is particularly important if you plan to move to the place. During your visit, weigh what you have learned about the place against what you observe. Don't hesitate to speak to the locals as well as government representatives and business men and women. Try to gain a full picture.

- If you are considering establishing a business, be sure to check the country's or jurisdiction's laws and business practices. Make certain that your company will be able to operate in the manner you anticipate. Particularly be certain that there will be solid markets for your company's products.

- Prior to signing any business agreements, have your attorney review them carefully. Ideally, your attorney should have ample experience and familiarity with international business practices.

- Finally, before committing yourself to any investment that promises to reduce you taxes, evaluate it to be certain that you will, in fact, receive the tax benefits you expect.

From the days of the first societies, soon after a leader or government was established, taxes were established, too. In many respects, governments have an unquenchable thirst for taxes. The only way governments can raise large amounts of funds is through taxation. Since taxes provide the funds for virtually all of a government's programs, and it often seems to be the nature of governments to expand programs (in an effort to improve them or provide more benefits for the program's beneficiaries), there is constant pressure to increase taxes. In its quest to obtain as much tax revenue as possible, the typical government will tax as many things as it can. Certainly, taxes on income, capital gains, real estate, sales, and inheritance are some of the most familiar taxes, however, many other taxes fall under the categories of licenses, registrations, user fees, and permits. It is the general position of government to resist efforts at tax reduction, unless forced by the demands of its citizens. Even then, many governments stand against the pressure for as long as possible.

Just about everyone pays too much in taxes. Even if you believe you have taken all the steps you can to minimize your tax obligations, if you have not considered the benefits and advantages offered by the countries and jurisdictions that are contained in this report, you have not done enough. Just think how much more of your money you would be able to spend for yourself and your family if you were able to reduce your taxes by 25%. Imagine if you could cut your taxes in half. Now consider eliminating them completely. The following countries and jurisdictions, found throughout the world, offer you the chance to significantly reduce your tax burdens, allowing you to keep more of your hard-earned money.

The Principality of Andorra

About half the size of New York City, the Principality of Andorra is located in the eastern region of the Pyrenees Mountains between France and Spain. The land of Andorra is rugged, highlighted by narrow valleys that cut between mountain peaks that reach elevations of 8,850 feet (2,700 meters). Great stretches of forests cover the mountains, except for the highest summits that overlook pastures of grazing sheep.

About 65,000 people live in Andorra. About 61% of the population is Spanish, 30% is native Andorran (who are Catalan in language and descent), and 6% is French. Although less than a third of the people consider themselves to be of Catalan descent, Catalan nevertheless is the official language. French and Castillian are also commonly spoken. The populace is well educated, the principality having a literacy rate of 99%, and Andorrans benefit from a quality system of health care. Andorra is, by all measures, a modern country.

Andorra: Yesterday and Today

Andorra's history can be traced to the 9th century when Charlemagne, king of the Franks, decreed that Andorra was to be a free state. Although the early historical record is sketchy, it is generally accepted that Andorra maintained its freedom until 1278 when the region fell under the shared authority of the Catalan Bishop of Urgel and the Count of Foix of France. Eventually, through the count, French kings and chiefs of state assumed the right to govern Andorra. France maintained control until March of

1993 when Andorrans voted to adopt a parliamentary system of government. Andorra's parliament provides its citizens with a stable government.

The principality is a rather delightful place. Its small area, nestled between the eastern Pyrenees, provides a large degree of isolation, which, coupled with the small population, creates an atmosphere devoid of the typical problems that beset bigger countries. Andorra la Vella, the capital city (population 19,500), is less like a city than a small town. Virtually everything is done in a leisurely fashion.

There are plenty of places to visit in Andorra. Huge mountains towering over Andorra la Vella provide a scene some people only see on postcards. The city boasts numerous discos that remain open throughout much of the night, various sites of impressive architecture such as the Chapel of St. Andreu, and a jazz festival hosted in July. A number of picturesque villages are scattered throughout the valleys and may be reached easily from the capital.

To enter Andorra, you will need a passport, but a visa is not required for business or tourist stays of up to three months. Further information about Andorra's entry requirements can be obtained from the Andorran Mission to the U.N., 212-750-8064.

Those unfamiliar with Andorra might be fooled by its size and think that the principality has less to offer than other places. Andorra is a modern and prosperous state that has something to offer to just about anyone.

At the center of Andorra's economy is skiing, with winter skiing perhaps being the principality's most popular pastime. While many tourists are drawn to Andorra's magnificent slopes in winter, many others are attracted to the cool and pleasing climate of summer.

Andorra also boasts a duty-free port, which alone attracts several million tourists each year. Goods from throughout Europe and as far away as Asia can be purchased at attractive prices. Extremely competitive prices may be found in clothing shops, jewelry shops, sports stores, boutiques, and opticians. About 4,000 shops vie for the consumer's interest. A new agreement with the European Union on duty-free allowances has significantly extended the values of duty-free products that may be bought in the principality and then taken to countries of the EU. Without question, Andorra is a thriving economic center.

Benefit of Andorra's Tax System

For individuals who are seeking a jurisdiction where they can substantially reduce or even eliminate their income taxes, Andorra should be high on their list. Andorra has no income taxes. This is clearly a significant benefit for almost all tax payers.

For more information about the Principality of Andorra, contact:

Andorran Mission to the United States
2 U.N. Plaza, 25th Floor
New York, NY 10018
Tel: 212-750-8064

The U.S. Consulate in Barcelona
Paseo Reina Elisenda 23-25
Barcelona
Spain
Tel: 34-3-280-2227

Department of Tourism
Prat de la Creu, 62
Andorra la Vella
Tel: 82-93-45
Fax: 86-01-84

There is also a private firm in Andorra which specializes in assisting prospective and current residents. They offer assistance with rental and purchase of apartments and homes, with residence permits, driver's licenses, car registration, mail handling in your absence, and many other things. I have spent many hours visiting with their managing director at their offices, and am impressed with the depth of knowledge of the country and the quality of their services. For more information contact:

Servissim
Edifici Areny, Baixos
Carretera General
Arinsal, La Massana
Principat d'Andorra
telephone: +376 837836
fax: +376 837179

<u>Anguilla</u>

A dependency of Great Britain that enjoys self-government, the coral island of Anguilla is located at the northern end of the Leeward Islands in the Caribbean. Anguilla is a low-lying, long and narrow island of about 35 square miles (90 square kilometers), with a maximum elevation of only about 200 feet (60 meters).

The island's tropical, semiarid climate and beautiful beaches make it a prime destination of tourists. Unlike many Caribbean islands that attract tourists by maintaining an energetic and exotic atmosphere, the residents and visitors of Anguilla enjoy tranquil days and relaxing, quiet nights. Anguilla, however, is far from a boring out-of-the- way island; various activities are enjoyed including swimming, snorkeling, boating, and fishing. The island has several excellent hotels and restaurants.

Anguilla: Yesterday and Today

Although Christopher Columbus discovered Anguilla in 1493, the island was not settled by Europeans until 1650 when the British founded a colony there. For much of its modern history, Anguilla was administrated as a part of St. Kitts-Nevis-Anguilla. Social upheaval in 1967 resulted in eventual British intervention. Upon bringing order back to the island, the British made Anguilla a dependency of the Crown while permitting the island to have its own government. Anguilla's dependency status was formalized in 1980 by the Anguilla Act. Since then Anguilla has enjoyed political and social stability.

British influence may be found just about everywhere on the island, with British architecture being most common in the capital, called The Valley. Although most of the island's residents are of African descent, English is the official language, the island's laws are based on British common law, and the civil service is based on the British model. Health care is considered good, as is education. The island's infrastructure, maintained principally by the British, is solid.

As one would expect, Anguilla's economy is based on tourism. With little industry on the island, many residents farm and fish.

Benefits of Anguilla's Tax System

Anguilla is truly one of the world's foremost tax havens. The island's tax code does not call for income taxes, corporate taxes, sales taxes, value added taxes, capital gains taxes, or taxes on interest.

The island's revenues necessary to maintaining governmental functions are raised through taxes on hotels, which are indirectly paid by tourists, import taxes, taxes on the sale of land sold to foreigners, and a lottery. British aid also helps support the island government.

For further information about Anguilla, contact:

The Anguilla Tourist Board
World Trade Centre
Suite 250
San Francisco, CA 94111
Tel: 415-398-3231
Fax: 415-398-3669

Anguilla Tourist Board
P.O. Box 1388
The Valley
Anguilla
Tel: 809-497-2759 or 800-553-4939
Fax: 809-497-2710

Anguilla Tourist Board
Windotel
3 Epirus Road
London SW6 7UJ
Great Britain
Tel: 011-441-71-937-7725
Fax: 011-441-71-938-4793

Antigua and Barbuda

An independent island country in the West Indies, Antigua and Barbuda are located east southeast of Puerto Rico. Three islands comprise the country: Antigua, Barbuda, and an uninhabited rocky islet, Redonda, that lies to the southwest. The island nation's area is small, only about two and a half times the size of Washington, D.C., or about 170 square miles (440 square kilometers). Antigua's highest point is Boggy Peak, about 1,330 feet (405 meters) high, but most of the island is near sea level. Barbuda is a coral island and generally flat. The islands lie within the tropics and enjoy pleasant Caribbean temperatures year-round.

Of the island nation's total population of 66,000, most have descended from Africans, British, Portuguese, Syrians, and Lebanese. About 27,000 people live in St. John's, the capital, and the islands' principal city.

Antigua and Barbuda: Yesterday and Today

Because the islands have been closely linked to Great Britain since 1632 when a group of Englishmen from St. Kitts established a successful settlement, much of the islands' traditions and customs are decidedly British. This is reflected in English being the country's official language (though local dialects are also widely spoken), and Anglicanism being the major religion. Other Protestant groups and also Roman Catholicism account for much of the other religious activity.

It wasn't long after the initial settlement that Antigua and Barbuda became major centers of the sugar industry. Indeed, it was the potential profits of growing sugar that drew many of the first colonists to the islands. By the end of the 18th century, however, Antigua had evolved into a vital strategic port as well as commercial center. Called the *"Gateway to the Caribbean,"* Antigua's location gave it control over major sailing routes throughout the islands of the region. It had become a valuable colony to the British.

Antigua remained firmly within the British sphere until 1981, when it gained its independence as Antigua and Barbuda. Although the island nation is independent, it retains close ties to the United Kingdom, as well as to the United States. The country's parliamentary government and legal system draw heavily from the British. In part because of the influence of Great Britain, Antigua and Barbuda are politically and socially stable. The islands are generally free from crime.

The economy of Antigua and Barbuda relies heavily on tourism. A variety of recreational activities are popular, including: boating, cricket, tennis, diving and snorkeling, windsurfing, hiking, golfing, fishing, swimming, and riding. Numerous nightclubs and fine restaurants are found on the islands, especially in St. John's, the capital. Shopping is a delightful pastime for many, and one can spend hours in the capital's shops and boutiques.

The islands' infrastructure is sound, and residents of the islands have access to all the conveniences of any modern country. Several major banks — including Antigua and Barbuda Development Bank, Bank of Antigua, Bank of Nova Scotia, Barclays Bank PLC, Royal Bank of Canada, and Swiss American National Bank of Antigua — offer a variety of services.

The level of health care on Antigua and Barbuda is excellent. The islands contain a hospital, private clinic, and several doctors, including specialists.

In many respects Antigua and Barbuda are island paradises. Scenic, picturesque, the lure of a relaxed, yet full and rich lifestyle, Antigua and Barbuda also offer significant tax advantages.

Benefit of Antigua and Barbuda's Tax System

Because much of the revenue of the islands comes from tourism, Antigua and Barbuda do not tax personal income. For those individuals who are seeking a way to eliminate income taxes, Antigua and Barbuda surely are worthy of consideration.

For additional information about Antigua and Barbuda, contact the following:

> **Antigua and Barbuda Department of Tourism**
> Long and Thames Streets
> P.O. Box 363
> St. John's
> Antigua, W.I.
> Tel: 268-462-0480
> Fax: 268-462-2483

> **Antigua and Barbuda**
> Chief of Mission
> 3216 New Mexico Ave., NW
> Washington, D.C. 20016
> Tel: 202-362-5211, 5166, 5122
> Fax: 202-362-5225

Antigua and Barbuda
Department of Tourism and Trade
25 S.E. 2nd Ave., Suite 300
Miami, FL 33131
Tel: 305-381-6762
Fax: 305-381-7908

Antigua and Barbuda Department of Tourism
610 Fifth Ave., Suite 311
New York, NY 10020
Tel: 212-541-4117
Fax: 212-757-1607

Antigua and Barbuda Department of Tourism and Trade
60 St. Claire Ave. East, Suite 304
Toronto, Ontario
Canada M4T 1N5
Tel: 416-961-3085
Fax: 416-961-7218

Antigua and Barbuda Department of Tourism
Antigua House, 15 Thayer St.
London W1M 5LD
England
Tel: 071-486-7073/4/5
Fax: 071-486-9970

Antigua and Barbuda Department of Tourism
Thomasstr. 11
D-61348 Bad Homburg
Germany
Tel: 49-6172-21504
Fax: 49-6172-21513

Argentina

A large, roughly triangular country, Argentina covers much of the southern part of South America. Having an area of 1,068,120 square miles (2,766,899 square kilometers), Argentina stretches more than 2,000 miles (3,300 kilometers) north to south, while its widest east to west line is only slightly longer than 850 miles (1,380 kilometers). Its great area ensures that the country has various topography, including long expanses of plains, highlands, and rugged mountains. Mt. Aconcagua in the western part of the country is the highest mountain in the Western Hemisphere at 22,831 feet (6,959 meters). A coastline of over 1,600 miles (2,600 kilometers) provides Argentina with numerous ports.

Argentina's population is about 35,000,000. Close to 85% of the country's people live in or near the cities, with 30% of all Argentines living in or near Buenos Aires, the nation's capital. Unlike many of the nations of Latin American which have large populations of Mestizos or native Americans, about 80% of Argentina's people are descended from Spanish and Italian settlers and immigrants, with smaller percentages of the population descending from the French, British, Germans, Russians, and Poles who immigrated to the country.

Because the Spanish were the first Europeans to settle Argentina, making it a colony, much Spanish heritage is found throughout the country. Today, Spanish is the country's official language, and close to 90% of the people are Roman Catholic.

Given its size and varying elevations, Argentina has several climates, though most fall within the broad category of the temperate zone. Buenos Aires, for example, enjoys an average summer temperature of 74 degrees F (*23 degrees C*), and an average winter temperature of 49 degrees F (*9.5 degrees C*). Like the climate, precipitation also varies depending upon latitude and altitude, though in general, rainfall is higher in the north and lower in the south. Buenos Aires receives about 40 inches (100 centimeters) of rain annually, about the same as cities along the east coast of the U.S.

In recent years Argentina has pursued policies that have enabled it to modernize at an impressive rate. Its governmental services have become more efficient, its health care is of excellent quality, particularly in the major cities, and its literacy rate is 95%. People living in Argentina are able to enjoy a lifestyle that is comparable to some of the best around the world.

Argentina: Yesterday and Today

The Spanish established the first permanent settlement in Argentina in 1553. By the latter part of the century Spain had assumed complete control and retained Argentina as a colony until 1816. It was in that year that Argentina declared itself to be a free state, however, not until 1853 was a federal constitution based on the Constitution of the United States adopted. The Argentina of today is a stable federal republic.

For much of the 20th century, Argentina was considered to be a country of vast untapped natural resources. Political and social unrest, poor policy decisions, and ill-advised legislation all combined to undermine the nation's economy. All that has changed, however. Throughout the 1990s, Argentina has made excellent progress in building a strong economy. The government has privatized several major industries since the early 1990s, ushering in an era of free enterprise that has greatly stimulated the economy and business climate. The nation's leadership has also initiated a program of infrastructure modernization, focusing on telecommunications and transportation. Argentina's great natural resources, including natural gas, petroleum, minerals, and farmland, have also been developed in attempts of expanding and sustaining growth. In response to the development of its natural resources, the manufacturing sector has also experienced strong growth. As the economy has grown, the consumer base has prospered and the service sector has expanded to meet the increasing demands.

Argentina is positioned for continued growth. The country enjoys economic stability and low inflation. Its money, the peso, is easily convertible to U.S. dollars, and the Central Bank supports the nation's currency through policies of rigorous administration. In addition, along with Brazil, Paraguay, and Uruguay, Argentina is a member of **MERCOSUR**, the **"common market"** of South America.

Benefits of Argentina's Tax System

Argentina does not offer as many tax incentives as some other countries do, however, the benefits its tax code does provide are potentially significant to some individuals.

* Argentina does not tax income from foreign sources.

* Authors and book publishers benefit from exemptions from income tax.

In addition, because of Argentina's pro-business environment, the tax rate on company profits is 33%, which is relatively low in comparison to international standards.

Should you be interested in finding out more about Argentina, contact:

The Embassy of Argentina
1600 New Hampshire Ave., NW
Washington, D.C. 20009
Tel: 202-939-6400/31/33
Fax: 202-332-3171

Consulate General of Argentina in Atlanta
245 Peachtree Center Ave.
Suite 2101
Atlanta, GA 30303
Tel: 404-880-0805
Fax: 404-880-0806

Consulate General of Argentina in Chicago
205 N. Michigan Ave.
Suite 4209
Chicago, IL 60601-5968
Tel: 312-819-2610
Fax: 312-819-2626

Consulate General of Argentina in Houston
1990 S. Post Oak Blvd.
Suite 770
Houston, TX 77056
Tel: 713-871-8935/6
Fax: 713-871-0639

Consulate General of Argentina in Los Angeles
5055 Wilshire Blvd.
Suite 210
Los Angeles, CA 90036
Tel: 213-954-9233
Fax: 213-934-9076

Consulate General of Argentina in Miami
World Trade Center
800 Brickell Ave.
Penthouse One
Miami, FL 33131
Tel: 305-373-1889/7794
Fax: 305-371-7108

Consulate General of Argentina in New York
12 West 56th St.
New York, NY 10019
Tel: 212-603-0400
Fax: 212-397-3523

Aruba

Aruba, an island in the Lesser Antilles, not far from the Venezuelan coast, belongs to the Netherlands. With an area of only about 75 square miles (193 square kilometers), Aruba is a small island, far longer at 19 miles (30 kilometers) than it is wide at 5 miles (8 kilometers).

Aruba's tranquil climate is one of the most delightful of the entire Caribbean. The island's temperatures remain remarkably consistent throughout the year averaging between 85 and 95 degrees F (29 to 35 degrees C), refreshing trade winds blow constantly between 10 and 20 miles per hour (16 and 32 kilometers per hour), and rain comes in the form of occasional showers, most commonly in the late fall. Ocean temperatures hover around 82 degrees F (27 degrees C) throughout the year. Positioned well out of the hurricane zone, Aruba's residents need not worry about major storms.

While tourists are always present on the island, Aruba's year-round residents total about 67,000, comprised mostly of mixed European and Caribbean Indian ancestry. Although Dutch is the official language, English and Spanish are also spoken throughout the island. Papiamento, a mixture of Dutch, English, Spanish, and Portuguese, is also widely spoken. Most people on Aruba are Roman Catholics, however, Protestants, Jews, Hindus, and Muslims are also present. The standard of living and health care on the island are of excellent quality.

One is never lacking for delightful things to do in Aruba. Magnificent tropical beaches, abundant sunshine, and a lifestyle that offers numerous activities such as swimming, snorkeling, boating, sailing, horseback riding, fine dining, dancing in exciting clubs, and gambling make Aruba one of the most attractive islands of the Caribbean.

Aruba: Yesterday and Today

Although the Spaniard Alonso de Ojeda discovered Aruba in 1499, Spain had little interest in the island because of its lack of precious minerals and its relatively dry climate, which would not support large-scale agriculture. In 1636 the Dutch, who were attempting to expand their presence in the Caribbean, seized several islands from Spain, including Aruba. Except for a short period during the Napoleonic Wars, the island has remained under Dutch control. In 1996, the Dutch were prepared to give Aruba its independence, but the island government requested that the island remain a part of the Netherlands. The Dutch granted the request and today Aruba has full autonomy in its internal affairs, yet remains firmly within the Dutch sphere.

Dutch influence is found throughout the island. Aruba has inherited its government, laws, language, customs, and much of its architecture from the Dutch. Aruba is a stable, prosperous democracy.

Unlike many islands of the Caribbean that rely primarily on tourism for their revenues, Aruba has followed a plan of economic diversification. While tourism, of course, is a major sector of the economy, the government is actively promoting various other sectors, including: telecommunications, a financial services industry, and a freezone of Aruba. Aruba's economic growth has averaged 5% annually with an inflation rate of about 3%. The island's economy is supported with an excellent infrastructure, including superior port facilities and an airport that is designed to make Aruba a hub for Latin America. In addition, the island is expanding its information technology infrastructure.

Aruba's currency is the Aruban florin (Af). The florin fluctuates with the dollar on the world markets and is considered to be a stable currency. U.S. and Canadian dollars are widely accepted in Aruba, while other currencies are exchangeable at Aruban banks. Aruba has several banks which offer various services, and ATMs are found throughout Orangjestad, the capital. Major credit cards are accepted by all hotels, most merchants, major restaurants, and businesses.

In the past, Aruba was not considered to be a place favorable to efforts at tax reduction. Within the last few years, however, that has changed. Aruba has undertaken major initiatives to expand and diversify its economy, offering important incentives to investors.

Benefits of Aruba's Tax System

Aruba currently offers various significant tax incentives and inducements. Most are designed specifically to encourage investment in industries the government has deemed vital to Aruba's economy, particularly for the strengthening of the island's economic base and for stimulating exports. Consider the following:

- A non-traditional manufacturing company that has an initial investment of Af 100,000 may be entitled to the following for a period of ten fiscal years:

  - A corporate tax rate of 0%.

- An exemption from income tax on dividends that are paid to shareholders (however, the dividends must be paid within two years after the year the profit has been earned).

- An exemption from taxes on real estate.

- An exemption from import duties on building supplies for the company's facilities.

- An exemption from import duties on various materials, including machinery and equipment, that are to be used in production processes.

• Special incentives are available for the construction of hotels, provided the initial investment is at least A £1,000,000. The incentives may be granted for a period of up to 10 fiscal years.

- A corporate tax rate to 0% of the net taxable profit.

- An exemption from income tax on dividends paid to shareholders (however, the dividends must be paid within two years after the profit has been earned).

- An exemption from taxes on real estate.

- An exemption from import duties on materials required for construction, including the fixtures and furniture for the hotel.

• Incentives are also available for offshore trading and offshore banking companies for a period of 10 fiscal years.

- A corporate tax rate of 2.4% and 3%.

- Incentives are available for investment and royalty companies up to the year 1999.

    - A corporate tax rate of 2.4% and 3%.

- Incentives are available for shipping and aviation companies up to the year 2000.

    - A corporate tax rate of 7.73% and 9.66%.

Aruba's freezone provides special incentives. Located in the vicinity of the Orangjestad Harbor and Barcadera, the freezone has been developed to provide facilities for industrial and commercial operations that may support the development of international trade. There are some restrictions to operation in the freezone however. Only a limited liability company that has been founded under Aruban law specifically for operation in the freezone is allowed to conduct business in the zone. A company can gain admittance to the zone if its operations are expected to aid Aruba's development into an international production, distribution, or service center. The following incentives apply:

- Profits earned from exports are taxed at 2%.

- Goods imported into the free zone, which are destined for re-exporting, are free of any duties.

Aruba also offers tax reductions to individuals.

- A nonresident shareholder of an Aruban offshore company is not subject to personal income tax on dividends, interest, liquidation distribution, or any other payments received from the company.

- A nonresident shareholder is not subject to income tax on capital gains on the disposal of his participation in an Aruban offshore company.

- Aruba has no withholding tax on capital and the taxpayer is not required to declare capital.

- Taxes are not charged on dividends or interest.

Although Aruba's tax exemptions and reductions generally apply to investors, many of its incentives can result in substantial tax savings. For more information about Aruba, contact:

Aruba Tourism Authority
L.G. Smith Blvd. 172
Eagle, Aruba
Dutch Caribbean
Tel: 2978-23777
Fax: 2978-34702

Aruba Tourism Authority
1000 Harbor Blvd.
Weehawken, NJ 07087
Tel: 201-330-0800 or 800-TO-ARUBA
Fax: 201-330-8757

Aruba Tourism Authority
1101 Juniper St., N.E.
Suite 1101
Atlanta, GA 30309-7627
Tel: 404-89-ARUBA
Fax: 404-873-2193

Aruba Tourism Authority
5901 North Cicero
Suite 301
Chicago, IL 60646
Tel: 773-202-5054
Fax: 773-202-9293

Aruba Tourism Authority
1 Financial Plaza
Suite 136
Ft. Lauderdale, FL 33394
Tel: 954-767-6477
Fax: 954-767-0432

Aruba Tourism Authority
12707 North Freeway
Ste. 138
Houston, TX 77060-1234
Tel: 281-87-ARUBA
Fax: 281-872-7872

Aruba Tourism Authority
86 Bloor St., West
Ste. 204
Toronto, Ontario M5S 1M5
Canada
Tel: 416-975-1950
Fax: 416-975-1947

Aruba Tourism Authority
Schimmelpennincklaan 1
2517 JN - The Hague
The Netherlands
Tel: 70-356-6220
Fax: 70-360-4877

Free Zone Aruba (FZA), N.V.
Schotlandstraat #49
Aruba
Dutch Caribbean
Tel: 297-820909
Fax: 297-820888

Aruba Financial Center
High Commissioner
Schotlandstraat #49
Aruba
Dutch Caribbean
Tel: 297-834611
Fax: 297-834665

The Azores

Centrally located between the Americas and Europe, the island group known as the Azores offer benefits to investors seeking ways to reduce their tax load. Nine major islands and several islets comprise the Azores, covering a distance of some 400 miles (644 kilometers) with a total land area of 902 square miles (2,334 square kilometers). The major islands are divided into three groups:

1. Eastern Group, which includes Sao Miguel (the largest island in size and population) and Santa Maria.

2. Central Group, which includes Terceira, Graciosa, Sao Jorge, Pico, and Faial.

3. Western Group, which includes Flores and Corvo.

The islands, which are an autonomous region of Portugal, are also divided into three administrative districts each with its own capital: Ponta Delgada on Sao Miguel, Horta on Faial, and Angra do Heroismo on Terceira. Each of the capitals is also a major seaport.

The warm waters of the Gulf Stream which flow past the islands provide the Azores with a temperate oceanic climate. Temperature varies little throughout the year, averaging 68 degrees F (20 degrees C) in summer and 54 degrees F (13 degrees C) in winter. Rainfall is ample throughout the year, which, combined with the mild climate, supports an abundant variety of vegetation.

Having formed from volcanoes that rose up from the sea long ago, the Azores are somewhat mountainous, with the highest peak being Pico Alto at 7,611 feet (2,320 meters). Although Pico Alto is still an active volcano, most of the volcanoes that created the islands have long been extinct.

The Azores have a population of about 260,000 people, of which about 75% live on Terceira and Sao Miguel. Much Portuguese influence is found throughout the islands, however, a large portion of the population has descended from various European groups as well as the Americas, resulting in a culture that contains much diversity within the general Portuguese culture. The overall population is a mixture from various ethnic groups.

The quality of life on the islands is good. Health care is on a standard of Europe, and education is available both through public and private schools. Indeed, private schools are found in many of the major cities and provide services for the children of many foreign residents.

The Azores: Yesterday and Today

Although historical records indicate that the Europeans knew about the Azores by the 1350s, it was not until 1427 that the Portuguese explored the islands to any extent, and not until 1445 that settlement began.

Their strategic location ensured the importance of the islands from the earliest days of New World colonization. For many years European ships traveling to and from the Indies stopped at the islands to pick up needed supplies. The islands later served as a place for Portuguese exiles.

During World War II the Azores were a vital Allied base, and today they serve as an operations base for the North Atlantic Treaty Organization (NATO).

There are many facets to the economy of the Azores. Taking advantage of their strategic position, tourism and export-related products are important sectors. Agricultural products, much of which are exported, are also vital. Because of the relatively small domestic population, manufacturing is limited to mostly food-related processes such as milling and bread-making, fish canning, and sugar products. Fishing is yet another important sector of the economy, with much of the population involved in fishing or related industries.

In recent years, the administrators of the islands have sought to increase trade as a fuel for economic growth. Realizing that trade relies largely on a solid infrastructure, the islands have taken steps to improve their ports, airports, and telecommunications system, all of which are now considered to be quite good.

Benefits of the Azores' Tax System

The tax system of the Azores is similar to the tax system of Portugal. While there are various taxes that must be paid, including professional tax, industrial tax, complementary tax, withholding tax, and real estate transfer tax, the islands enjoy an important advantage over Portugal and many other countries in regard to their Value Added Tax (VAT). In Portugal, the rate for the VAT is over 40%, while in the Azores it is 12%. This can be a significant advantage for some investors.

Investors should also consider the various investment incentives that the Azores offer, which often include significant packages of financial aid, subsidies, and interest-free loans.

Should you wish to learn more about the Azores, contact the following:

Regional Tourism Board
Casa do Relogio
Colonia Alema
9900 Horta
Azores
Tel: +351-0-92-23801/2/3/4
Fax: +351-0-92-22004

Chamber of Commerce and Industry of the Azores
Rua Ernesto do Canto, 13
9500 Ponta Delgada
Azores
Tel: +351-0-96-22427, 23235, 25408, or 27589
Fax: +351-0-96-24268

Instituto de Investimento e Privatizacoes dos Acores
Praca 5 de Outubro, 12
9500 Ponta Delgada
Azores
Tel: +351-0-96-25427
Fax: +351-0-96-25349

Camara do Comercio de Angra do Heroismo
Rua da Palha, 32/34
9700 Angra do Heroismo
Azores
Tel: +351-0-96-23470
Fax: +351-0-96-27131

The Bahamas

Most people think of The Bahamas as an island playground where tourism is king. They don't realize that The Bahamas also have a tax code that offers many benefits.

Beginning about 50 miles (80 kilometers) from the Florida coast, the large group of islands and islets that comprise The Bahamas cover thousands of square miles, all the way to nearly 60 miles (96 kilometers) off the coast of Cuba. While thirty of the islands are inhabited, thousands of islets that are a part of the group are not. The overall area of The Bahamas is about 5,400 square miles (13,900 square kilometers). The islands possess some of the world's most spectacular beaches, as well as offering an exotic lifestyle, particularly on Nassau.

One of the reasons for the popularity of The Bahamas as vacation spot is the delightful climate that is summer-like throughout the year. The average summer temperature ranges between 70 and 80 degrees F (*21 and 27 degrees C*), while in winter the night's temperatures may fall to about 60 degrees F (*16 degrees C*). Rain comes in the form of showers that interrupt the otherwise abundant sunshine. Usually coming in the early morning or late afternoon, the rain seldom lasts long.

About 273,000 people live on the islands. People of African descent comprise about 85% of the population, with the rest of the population being originally British, Canadian, or American. English is the dominant language with Creole also widely spoken. While most of the people on the islands belong to Protestant churches, Roman Catholics are also well represented.

The people of The Bahamas enjoy a high standard of living. Health care is excellent, the literacy rate is 98%, and the islands' infrastructure is excellent. Various water activities, an exciting nightlife, fine restaurants, shopping, and quiet, out-of-the-way spots for simply relaxing combine to create an atmosphere that is unique in the world.

The Bahamas: Yesterday and Today

Throughout the years that European explorers searched out the islands of the New World, many set foot on the islands that were to become The Bahamas. In 1647 the British established the first settlement and in 1783 The Bahamas became a British colony, remaining a possession of the Crown until 1964 when the islands were granted internal self-government. In 1973 The Bahamas attained full independence but remain a member of the Commonwealth.

British influence is found throughout the islands. Although the chief of state is the British monarch, the actual leader of the government is the prime minister who governs The Bahamas with the help of a bicameral parliament. The government and laws of The Bahamas are based on those of England.

Because of the breathtaking beauty of the islands and their wonderful climate, the economy is built around tourism, which accounts for close to half of The Bahamas GDP. Other major sectors of the economy include banking, pharmaceuticals, and rum production. The infrastructure of the islands is one of the most advanced of all the islands in the hemisphere. By all accounts, The Bahamas are an excellent place to live and work.

Benefits of The Bahamas' Tax System

Because The Bahamas obtain much of their revenue from import duties, their tax code is generous in the advantages it offers. Individuals interested in reducing their tax burdens should review the following:

- The Bahamas have no income tax.

- There are no estate or inheritance taxes.

- There are no death duties in respect of real or personal estates.

- There are no income taxes on companies.

- There are no dividend taxes.

- There are no gift taxes.

If you would like to find out more information about The Bahamas, contact the following:

The Bahamas Tourism Office
150 E. 52nd St.
28th Floor North
New York, NY 10022
Tel: 212-758-2777
Fax: 212-753-6531

The Bahamas Tourism Office
2957 Clairmont Rd.
Suite 150
Atlanta, GA 30329
Tel: 404-633-1793
Fax: 404-633-1575

Embassy of The Bahamas
2220 Massachusetts Ave., NW
Washington, DC 20008
Tel: 202-319-2660
Fax: 202-319-2668

The Bahamas Tourism Office
P.O. Box N 3701
Nassau
The Bahamas
Tel: 242-322-7500
Fax: 242-328-0945

The Bahamas Tourism Office
3, The Billings
Walnut Tree Close
Guilford, Surrey GUI 4UL
England
Tel: 01483-448900
Fax: 01483-448990

Barbados

Located in the Windward Islands of the Lesser Antilles, Barbados is the most easterly of the islands in the Caribbean. Barbados is larger than many islands of the Western Hemisphere with an area of about 165 square miles (430 square kilometers). Possessing a flat outer rim along the coast, the island's interior is comprised of hills with its highest point, Mt. Hillaby, rising to 1,104 feet (336 meters).

Well within the tropics, but freshened by the near constant but gentle breeze of the Northeast Trade Winds, the average annual temperature of Barbados is about 79 degrees F (*26 degrees C*). Along with cooling the island, the winds also lessen the humidity, giving Barbados a lower average summer time humidity than many of the cities of North America. Although a rainy season occurs from June to November, the island receives an abundant amount of sunshine, resulting in the island's being a prime tourist resort.

Because Barbados lacks mineral resources, the island government has established legislation designed to attract investment. Barbados offers a variety of tax and other incentives to investors. While many of these inducements are related to the founding of a business on the island, they are significant and provide the possibility of major tax savings.

About 260,000 people live year-round in Barbados, though the actual number of people on the island at any given time is larger due to the numbers of tourists that are always present. More than half of the residents live along the Caribbean coast in a large generally urban area that extends from Speightstown in the north to Oisten in the south and St. Philip in the east. The rest of Barbados's people live in small towns, villages, and hamlets located throughout the island.

The people of Barbados enjoy a high standard of living. The educational system has produced a literacy rate of 98%, the system of health care is of high quality, and per capita income ranks as one of the best in the entire Caribbean. Indeed, in a recent United Nations report that analyzes levels of education, per capita income, and life expectancy, Barbados was rated first among developing countries. Perhaps an even better indicator of the standard of living in Barbados is the island's 20th ranking out of 160 developed countries on the United Nation's Human Development Index.

About 90% of the island's population is descended from Africans, with the remainder composed of whites and persons of mixed descent. English is the official language. Most of the people are Anglican, however, there are large numbers of people belonging to other Protestant sects and Roman Catholicism.

Barbados offers its people an excellent lifestyle. People are open and friendly, racial and ethnic tensions are rare or nonexistent, and the crime rate is low. Recreational activities include swimming on pristine beaches, sailing, boating, fishing, golf, tennis, cycling, hiking, horseback riding, and cricket. Grand hotels and restaurants serve excellent food, theater groups stage quality productions, and the music of the island is an attraction for all. Moreover, a variety of annual festivals are enjoyed by island dwellers and tourists alike.

Barbados: Yesterday and Today

The Portuguese were the first Europeans to explore Barbados. When they began stopping at the island around the mid 1530s, they found little of interest. They did give the island its name, however — Los Barbados, named by sailors after the aerial roots of the island's ficus trees which they thought resembled beards.

As late as 1625 the island was uninhabited. In that year the English Captain John Powell landed on Barbados and claimed it for England. Two years later English settlers arrived. Not long afterward, sugar cane was introduced to the island and quickly became a major crop. The lure of a new life, a thriving sugar cane farm, and Barbados's wonderful climate resulted in a rapid increase in population. Having assumed English laws and customs that are present today, the island soon was referred to as "Little England."

Even though Barbados became independent from Great Britain in 1966, the island remains within the British Commonwealth. The constitution of 1966 created a parliament and prime minister modeled closely on the executive and legislative branch of government in England. Barbados's judicial system is modeled on English common law. Unlike many of the islands of the Caribbean which have experienced political and social unrest, Barbados has been an example of a stable democracy.

This stability has enabled the government of the island to develop a plan with which to diversify the island's economy. In the past, sugar cane and rum were the major sectors of Barbados's economy, while today tourism, information and financial services, and light manufacturing combine with traditional agriculture to support a healthy economic environment.

In an effort to maintain its competitive edge — which includes a well-educated workforce, extremely attractive wages, and low taxes — island authorities have invested heavily in maintaining a modern infrastructure. Barbados's air and seaport facilities, its roads, and telecommunications are of excellent quality. Its telecommunications systems are on a par with those of the United States, a result of which has been the emergence of Barbados as the major communications center in the eastern Caribbean.

Barbados has also developed into an important financial center in the Caribbean. The Caribbean Development Bank maintains its headquarters at Barbados, providing services throughout the region. A sophisticated financial system made up of banks, finance companies, trust companies, insurance companies, a mortgage company, a number of credit unions, and the Barbados Development Bank provide individuals and businesses with all the services they need. Overseeing the financial system of the island and insuring the island's financial base is the Central Bank of Barbados. The duties of the bank are significant: issuing currency, managing foreign assets, monitoring exchange controls, supervising commercial banks and other financial institutions, as well as controlling the government's capital markets.

Benefits of Barbados's Tax System

To attract investment to Barbados, the government of the island has passed legislation that provides for various tax incentives.

While many of the inducements are designed for businesses, individuals may also benefit. Tax incentives for foreign investors are noted in the International Business Companies Act 1991-24, the most significant of which are noted below:

- A tax rate of 2.5% on profits.

- Exemptions from all local taxes on dividends, interest, fees, royalties, management fees, or other incomes paid to non-residents.

- Exemptions from local taxes on transfers of securities or assets, except for real property located in Barbados or for equipment used on the island.

- Exemptions from taxes and duties on machinery, computer equipment, raw materials, goods, or other articles imported into Barbados.

- Exemption from exchange controls.

- Exemption from public filing of financial statements.

- A guarantee of the above benefits for a period of 15 years.

A key to your tax status in Barbados is the definitions of "resident" and "domiciled." An individual who is resident and domiciled in Barbados is liable to pay income tax on his or her worldwide income. It doesn't matter whether the income is remitted to Barbados. To be considered a resident of the island, you must be present in Barbados for more than 182 days in a tax year. An individual who is resident, but not domiciled in Barbados must pay tax on income derived from Barbados as well as any overseas income remitted to Barbados. However, nonresidents are responsible for paying tax only on income derived from Barbados. Any incentives that an individual may be eligible for can significantly reduce his or her tax payments.

Individuals may also realize important tax savings through the establishment of a business in Barbados.

For companies that provide information services the following incentives are available:

- For data entry operations that conduct their business in international markets, a tax rate of 2.5% on net profits.

- Exemptions from import tariffs on equipment related to production.

- Other non-tax incentives include cash grants for training, subsidized space in one of the island's ten industrial parks, the possibility of an accelerated depreciation allowance, and full and unrestricted repatriation of capital, profits, and dividends.

For investment in manufacturing and export industries, the following incentives may be applicable:

- An exemption on corporate profits for up to 10 years.

- Upon expiration of the tax exemption, export industries may be eligible for a tax rate of 2.5%.

- An exemption from import duties on raw materials, equipment, and production machinery.

- Other non-tax incentives including the following —

  - Simplified custom procedures.

- Worker training grant program. (Employers may receive a reimbursement of up to 75% of the wages paid to trainees during the first six months of the operation of a business.

- Free coordination for procedures regarding investment, resulting in a decrease of "red tape."

International service companies that establish offshore operations in Barbados may be entitled to the following:

- A tax rate of 1 to 2.5% on the profits of investment companies.

- A tax rate of 2.5% for international business firms.

- A tax rate of 2.5% on the profits of information technology service companies.

- A full tax exemption for companies defined as **"captive insurance companies."**

- A full tax exemption for United States foreign sales corporations.

Should you like to learn more about Barbados, contact the following:

Barbados Investment and Development Corporation
800 Second Ave.
New York, NY 10017
Tel: 212-867-6420
Fax: 212-682-5496

Barbados Investment and Development Corporation
5160 Yonge St.
Suite 1800
North York, Ontario M2N 6L9
Tel: 416-512-0700
Fax: 416-512-6580

Barbados Investment and Development Corporation
Princess Alice Highway
Bridgetown, Barbados
West Indies
Tel: 809-427-5350
Fax: 809-426-7802

Bermuda

When most people think of Bermuda, they usually think of the Main Island, which is also known as Great Bermuda. Bermuda actually refers to a group of about 150 islands in the North Atlantic Ocean east of North Carolina. About 20 of the islands of Bermuda are inhabited, with Great Bermuda containing the greatest portion of the population. The overall area of the island group is about 20 square miles (53 square kilometers), about one-third the size of Washington, D.C. The islands of Bermuda don't rise much above sea level, though some are hilly.

Bermuda's subtropical climate is mild and humid, averaging near 70 degrees F (21 degrees C) in summer and about 63 degrees F (17 degrees C) in the winter. The islands' humidity is a result of their location in the Gulf Stream, which fosters southerly winds laden with moisture. The humidity accounts for Bermuda's average annual rainfall of about 58 inches (1470 centimeters), but the islands still manage to delight in an abundant amount of sunshine throughout the year. The climate, coupled with the Bermuda's lush vegetation and natural beauty, make Bermuda one of the prime vacation destinations of the world.

About 62,000 people are year-round residents, however, because of the great concentration of tourists, the number of people on the islands is usually much greater. Close to 60% of the population is black, while most of the rest are descended from white Europeans. English is the predominate language, and the islands have a literacy rate of 98%. Health care is excellent.

Bermuda is a dependent territory of the United Kingdom and has its capital at Hamilton. Since 1968 Bermuda has enjoyed internal self-government through a bicameral parliament. The chief of state is the British monarch, who appoints a governor for the islands. The governor appoints a premier, who then nominates individuals for a cabinet to assist him in carrying out his executive duties. Bermuda's laws are based on British common law.

Bermuda: Yesterday and Today

Named after a Spanish navigator — Juan de Bermudez — who was shipwrecked on one of the islands of the group in 1503, settlement didn't occur for nearly another 100 years, and it was English colonists who established the first footholds. English settlement was not planned, but was the result of another shipwreck, much like the one that had stranded Bermudez.

An English party, led by George Somers, had originally sailed for Virginia but was blown off course and landed in Bermuda in 1609. By 1612, the "Somers Islands" were a part of the third charter of the Virginia Company. Soon afterward a second group of colonists arrived. The original charter was revoked in 1684 and the islands were made a crown colony. As time passed, Somers Islands were more often referred to by the name of Bermuda, which is the name that finally gained general acceptance. Except for the history books, George Somers and his original colonists were forgotten.

Bermuda has developed into one of the world's most prosperous islands. Its GDP per capita of $28,000 is one of the highest in the world.

The islands' economy is built on the tourist industry, financial services, pharmaceuticals, ship repair, paints, and concrete products. The islands possess a fully modern infrastructure that supports the economy and gives Bermuda a decided competitive edge over many of its neighbors. The islands' currency is the Bermudian dollar, which equals the U.S. dollar; it is a stable currency and is maintained at a fixed rate.

There is little question that Bermuda is an exceptional island that offers a truly wonderful lifestyle. A little known fact about Bermuda, perhaps because it is overshadowed by the glitz of a vacation mecca, is that the dependency also offers significant tax advantages.

Benefit of Bermuda's Tax System

Bermuda offers various tax benefits, including:

- Bermuda has no income tax.

- Bermuda does not tax personal or corporate profits.

- Bermuda does not tax dividends, personal or corporate.

- There are no capital gains taxes.

- There are no withholding taxes.

- There are no gift taxes.

- International companies that are registered in Bermuda may apply for an exemption from taxes on profits or income until the year 2016 in the event that such taxes are ever implemented in Bermuda.

(**Note**: Exempted companies may be owned up to 100% by individuals or entities that are not Bermudian.)

Other advantages that Bermuda offers investors include:

- Political stability.

- Economic stability.

- Legislation supportive of business and investment.

- Minimal amount of bureaucracy and government intervention.

- Solid, modern infrastructure, considered by many to be the most developed of all offshore jurisdictions.

- Modern communications.

- Lack of exchange controls.

- Proximity to the NAFTA markets.

- Reputation for high standards in the conduct of business.

For many individuals who are seeking ways to reduce their tax burdens, residency in Bermuda can lead to important savings on tax requirements. Even international companies may benefit from Bermuda's tax code.

If there is a downside to all this, unfortunately, it is difficult to obtain a residency permit in Bermuda, and it is expensive to settle in the islands. It is usually required that a resident buy property in value upwards to at least a million dollars. Nevertheless, for investors with the necessary assets, Bermuda can provide the means for reducing taxes and building wealth.

Should you like to learn more about Bermuda, contact the following:

The Bermuda Tourism Office
Global House
43 Church St.
Hamilton, HM 11
Bermuda
Tel: 441-292-0023
Fax: 441-292-7537

Bermuda Department of Tourism
310 Madison Ave.
Suite 201
New York, NY 10017
Tel: 212-818-9800 or 800-223-6106 or 800-Bermuda

Bermuda Department of Tourism
245 Peachtree Center, Ave., NE
Suite 803
Atlanta, GA 30303
Tel: 404-524-1541

Bermuda Department of Tourism
1200 Bay St.
Suite 1004
Toronto, M5R 2A5
Canada
Tel: 416-923-9600

Bermuda Department of Tourism
1 Battersea Church Rd.
London, SW11 3LY
England
Tel: 171-743-8813

Bermuda Department of Tourism
Herzogspitalstrasse 5 80331
Munich
Germany
Tel: 011-49-892-67874

Bolivia

A landlocked country in central South America, Bolivia welcomes foreign investment and, particularly during the last 10 years, has offered various incentives to attract international investors. Bolivia is a large nation, about 424,000 square miles (1,098,500 square kilometers), and possesses varying topography, including lowlands, plains, plateaus, and mountains. An impressive central plateau that averages 12,000 feet in elevation (3,600 meters) is situated between two mountain ranges that boast three of the highest peaks in South America. On the Peruvian border lies Lake Titicaca, the highest lake in the world at 12,056 feet (3,616 meters). The lowlands of the east-central region of the country are covered with semitropical forests.

As would be expected of an expansive land that has such great contrasts in elevation, Bolivia's has many climate zones, closely linked to its geography. Low-lying regions are generally warm, especially as one moves northward closer to the equator, while the plateaus and mountain areas have temperate climates. Some of the highest mountains in the southern part of the country have cold climates. Average temperatures also vary, from about 47 degrees F (*8 degrees C*) in the highlands to about 80 degrees F (*26 degrees C*) in the lowlands. Rainfall, too, varies, depending on the region but is usually ample. By far, much of the country experiences a temperate climate that has neither great extremes of high and low temperatures, or precipitation.

Slightly more than 7.7 million people live in Bolivia. Most speak Spanish, but because the country possesses a rather large native Indian population, Quechua and Aymara are also official languages. About 40% of the Indian population is not thought to speak Spanish, which is the preferred language of government, business, and education. Native Indians make up the largest ethnic groups, with 30% of the population being Quechua, 25% being Aymara, 30% being Mestizo, and the rest being European. By far, most of the population is Roman Catholic.

Unfortunately, Bolivia has not achieved the standard of living of many of its neighbors, and certainly not the level of advanced nations. About 80% of the population is literate, and health care, while adequate in the major cities, declines rapidly as one reaches outlying villages.

Bolivia: Yesterday and Today

The Spanish seized control of the land that was to become Bolivia in the 1530s, taking it from the Incas. Spain remained in control until 1825 when Bolivia gained its independence in a revolution led by Simon Bolivar, after whom the new nation took its name. Bolivia is a republic whose capital city is Sucre, but the government's headquarters are located in La Paz.

During much of its history, Bolivia has experienced military and social conflict, however, in recent years the government has taken major steps to achieve political stability on which it hopes to build a strong and growing economy. For years, Bolivia has been one of South America's poorest countries, a condition the government has attempted to rectify by introducing legislation that will provide a positive economic climate. In recent years, the government has taken actions to maintain fiscal discipline, support free-market policies, particularly through a privatization program, and modernize the country's infrastructure to increase the competitiveness of its industries and businesses.

Benefits of Bolivia's Tax System

Although Bolivia has a rather demanding tax system, there are opportunities for investors. Moreover, its tax rates are frequently lower than the rates of other countries. Note the following:

- Net income tax rate, 25%.

- Value added tax, 13%.

- In addition, special tax treatments and rates are available in depressed regions, such as Oruro and Potosi).

- Foreigner investors and nationals are eligible for the same tax reimbursements on exports.

Foreign investors may benefit from other incentives as well, including:

- No restrictions on capital flow, either in or out of the country, except for a remittance abroad tax of 12.5%.

- Freedom for the importing and exporting of all legal goods and services.

- Prior authorization or registration is not required for private investment, except for those conditions contained in the Commerce Code.

- The Bolivian currency, the Boliviano, is freely and easily convertible into foreign currency.

- There are essentially no restrictions to foreign investment in the country.

Although Bolivia may not offer big tax incentives like some jurisdictions, the country has a large consumer base with high expectations and pent-up demand products and services. Bolivia, clearly, is not the right investment choice for everyone, however, for some investors it offers the potential to not only reduce taxes but build a thriving business as well.

Should you be interested in learning more about Bolivia, contact the following:

The Bolivian Embassy
3014 Massachusetts Ave., NW
Washington, D.C. 20008
Tel: 202-483-4410 through 4412
Fax: 202-328-3712

American Chamber of Commerce of Bolivia
Av. 6 de Agosto
Edificio Hilda, Oficina 203
La Paz
Bolivia
Tel: 591-2-432573
Fax: 591-2-432472

National Chamber of Industry
Av. Mariscal Santa Cruz, N 1392
Edificio Camara Nacional de Comercio, piso 14
P.O. Box 7 LP
La Paz
Bolivia
Tel: 591-2-378606
Fax: 591-2-391004

Campione

Campione, formally referred to as Campione d'Italia, is a small Italian enclave surrounded by Switzerland. Located in the Swiss Canton of Ticino, on the eastern shore of Lake Lugano beneath a picturesque mountain, Campione lies about 16 miles from the Italian border. Although Campione is within Switzerland, there are no border controls and access in and out of the enclave is easy.

Campione is, unquestionably, in terms of borders and political affiliations, one of the more unique places in the world. The enclave is a part of Italy's Como province and is subject to Italian laws, however it conducts its daily life and routines in a manner more like it is a part of Switzerland. Campione residents use Swiss facilities such as the post office, banks, and telecommunications services. The official currency of the enclave is the Swiss franc, but the Italian lire is accepted as well (which will no doubt give way to the Euro). Driver's whose cars are registered in Campione even have Swiss license plates.

Of most interest to individuals seeking to reduce their tax obligations is the fact that the residents of Campione live under their own tax system, which is decidedly more beneficial than the tax codes of either Italy or Switzerland. Moreover, Campione offers an extremely attractive lifestyle. The enclave's 3,000 residents are well educated, enjoy fine health care, and may indulge themselves in various recreational activities including skiing, fishing, hiking, golf, fine restaurants, and water sports. A casino operated by the municipality itself provides excitement and entertainment, and just an hour's drive away is the Italian city of Milan, renowned for its cultural attractions. Of course, places to visit and enjoy in Switzerland are also nearby.

Campione: Yesterday and Today

Campione's unique status can be traced back to the 13th century when the Lord of Campione presented the village of Campione and its territory to the Church of St. Ambrosius of Milan. In the 18th century, Austria gained control of the enclave, and not long after that Campione was made a part of Italy, even though it was surrounded by Switzerland. Throughout all those years, Swiss authorities have accepted the state of Campione within their borders.

Being such a small municipality, Campione does not have a major economy; however, neither does it have the excessive expenses of big government. The enclave's economy is centered around its municipal casino and other recreational activities.

To obtain a residency permit, you must either own a house or rent an apartment or house. Compared to obtaining residency in Switzerland, or many other places, obtaining residency in Campione is not terribly difficult.

Benefits of Campione's Tax System

Campione offers numerous benefits to those who are seeking to reduce their tax burden. Consider the following:

- Campione has no personal income tax.

- There is no municipal tax.

- Residents of Campione are not subject to Switzerland's double taxation agreements with other nations. This includes most of the countries of Western Europe, the United States, and Canada.

- Campione has no value added tax (VAT).

Campione is politically, economically, and socially stable, and its residents enjoy a most attractive standard of living. Unlike many places that advertise their tax-haven benefits, providing information in an attempt to attract investors, Campione officials do not offer much information about the enclave. Your best strategy of finding out more about Campione, therefore, is to visit the enclave yourself.

The Cayman Islands

Halfway between Cuba and Honduras lie the three islands that comprise the Cayman Islands. Grand Cayman lies just northwest of Jamaica, and Little Cayman and Cayman Brac are located about 80 miles (130 kilometers) northeast of Grand Cayman. The total area of the three islands is about 100 square miles (260 square kilometers), or about one and a half times the area of Washington, D.C. Mostly low-lying, the highest point of the islands is known as the Bluff, which is only about 142 feet (43 meters) above sea level.

The Cayman Islands, which are a dependency of Great Britain, enjoy a tropical marine climate with fine summers and pleasant dry winters. Tourists are drawn to the spectacular beaches year-round.

The tourist population is a significant addition to the island's 35,000 residents. The resident population can be divided into the following groups: 40% are of mixed race, 20% are black, 20% are white, and 20% are of various ethnic groups. Most of the people are either Protestant or Catholic.

The Cayman islands offer an excellent standard of living. Health care is of high quality, the literacy rate is 98%, and the infrastructure of the islands is one of the best in the Caribbean. Various recreational activities are available, including: swimming, snorkeling, fishing, boating, shopping, fine dining and nightly entertainment. Of course, along with all this residents and visitors enjoy the tropical nature of the island.

While in the past the Cayman Islands were primarily a destination for vacationers, the islands have developed into a major international financial center that offers substantial benefits in regard to investment and taxes. Indeed, the investor who is seeking ways to increase the value of his portfolio while decreasing his tax exposure would be wise to consider the advantages the Cayman Islands offer.

The Cayman Islands: Yesterday and Today

Although Columbus was the first European to explore the Cayman Islands in 1503, Spain had little interest in colonizing them. It wasn't until 1734 that British colonists who came from Jamaica established the first settlement. The islands remained a British dependency until 1959. In that year they became a self-governing member of the Federation of the West Indies, however, dissatisfied with that arrangement, the islands' government asked Great Britain to reinstate dependency status, which it did in 1962. Since then, the Cayman Islands have remained a dependency of Great Britain, a situation that is agreeable to both sides.

British influence on the islands is pronounced. The government is based on the British Parliament, and the laws of the islands are based on British common law. The Cayman Islands are stable both socially and politically. There are no formal political parties on the islands.

The Cayman Islands boast one of the highest standards of living in the world. While an offshore financial center and tourism at the rate of close to a million visitors per year are the foundation of the economy, shipbuilding, construction, fishing, farming, and turtle raising are also important sectors of the economy. The infrastructure and telecommunications systems throughout the islands are excellent.

While the various sectors of the economy of the Cayman Islands combine to create an envious lifestyle, it is the financial sector that is of greatest interest to investors. The Cayman Islands are one of the top financial centers in the world. Over the last 25 years the jurisdiction has enacted legislation that encourages business and has produced a prime business environment. There are some 50 banks on the islands, with deposits of U.S. $415 billion. Of the world's top 50 banks, 46 are resident in Cayman, including Barclays, the Royal Bank of Canada, Bank of Butterfield, Bank of Nova Scotia, British American Bank, and the Cayman National Bank.

Attracted by the pro-business climate, about 3,000 new companies are formed in the Cayman Islands each year. Three types of companies comprise the bulk of the company formations. These include:

- Resident companies, the primary function of most being local trade.

- Non-resident companies, that are used for a variety of international activities.

- Exempted companies, which may be used for various operations, including offshore captive insurance and reinsurance purposes and cash management operations. (It is noteworthy that in the category of captive insurance, the Cayman Islands are second only to Bermuda in share of the global market.

Britannia Corporate Management, Ltd.

As many investors have already discovered, it can be difficult to find an independent company management service. Many of these services are provided by large banks and institutions, which often overlook or outright ignore the needs of individual investors.

Britannia Corporate Management, Ltd., which is based in the Cayman Islands, is an excellent alternative. The company is licensed by the government of the islands to incorporate and manage Cayman Island registered companies. The president of Britannia is Gary F. Oakley. A Canadian who has been a permanent resident of the Cayman Islands for over 17 years, he possesses substantial experience in financial management and offshore companies.

Britannia can be of enormous benefit to investors, for the company offers numerous services, including: provision of a registered office, corporate secretary, officers and directors, and the handling of the daily administration and management of the company's business. To this end, Britannia is licensed to manage various business activities such as investment holding and trading companies, life insurance holding companies, patent holding companies, and real estate holding companies. In addition, they manage invoicing and trading companies. Furthermore, as specified in the Cayman Islands Mutual Funds Law, Britannia is able to provide the registered office, and also the specialized management and administrative functions that are necessary to an offshore mutual fund.

If you would like to find out more about Britannia Corporate Management, Ltd., you may contact them at the following address:

Britannia Corporate Management, Ltd.
Attn: New Clients Information
P.O. Box 1968
Whitehall Estates, Grand Cayman
Cayman Islands
Fax: +1-345-949-0716, Attn: New Clients Information

Benefits of the Cayman Islands' Tax System

For residents of the Cayman Islands, there is no income tax or any other form of direct taxation.

In an effort to attract individuals of good character and financial resources to the islands, the government of the Cayman Islands has established policies that will facilitate residency applications. There are some conditions that must be met, including:

- An applicant for residency must be in a financial position in which he or she can invest in a home or local business in the Cayman Islands.

- The investment required must be equivalent to a minimum of U.S. $180,000.

Should you wish to find out more information about obtaining residency status in the Cayman Islands, contact the following:

The Chief Immigration Officer
Department of Immigration
P.O. Box 1098
Grand Cayman
B.W.I.

If you would like to learn more about the Cayman Islands, contact the following:

Cayman Islands Department of Tourism
The Pavilion
Cricket SquareGrand
P.O. Box 67 George Town
Grand Cayman
B.W.I.
Tel: 345-949-0623
Fax: 345-949-4053

Cayman Islands Department of Tourism
420 Lexington Ave.
Suite 2733
New York, NY 10170
Tel: 212-682-5582
Fax: 212-986-5123

Cayman Islands Department of Tourism
9525 W. Bryn Mawr
Suite 160
Rosemont, IL 60018
Tel: 847-678-6446
Fax: 847-678-6675

Cayman Islands Department of Tourism
Two Memorial City Plaza
820 Gessner
Suite 170
Houston, TX 77024
Tel: 713-461-1317
Fax: 713-461-7409

Cayman Islands Department of Tourism
6100 Blue Lagoon Dr.
Suite 150
Miami, FL 33126-2085
Tel: 305-266-2300
Fax: 305-267-2932

Cayman Islands Department of Tourism
3340 Wilshire Blvd.
Suite 1202
Los Angeles, CA 90010
Tel: 213-738-1968
Fax: 213-738-1829

Cayman Islands Department of Tourism
Travel Marketing Consultants
234 Eglinton Ave., East
Suite 306
Toronto, Ontario M4P1 K5
Canada
Tel: 416-485-1550
Fax: 416-485-7578

Cayman Islands Department of Tourism
6 Arlington St.
London, SW1A 1RE
England
United Kingdom
Tel: 0171-491-7771
Fax: 0171-409-7773

Ceuta and Melilla

Located on the coast of Morocco, and at first glance appearing that they should be a part of that nation, are the two small enclaves of Ceuta and Melilla. Though on the southern coast of the Mediterranean, the enclaves belong to Spain. While the enclaves don't offer tax incentives on a par with some other tax havens, their tax laws do provide important benefits. Moreover, other factors such as a duty-free port, growing economies, up-to-date infrastructures, and an enjoyable mild Mediterranean subtropical climate help to make Ceuta and Melilla potentially valuable jurisdictions in which to reduce your tax obligations.

The city of Ceuta — total area of about nine square miles (23 square kilometers) — lies on the Strait of Gibraltar in northwest Africa. It is located on the site of ancient Abila, considered by many historians to be one of the Pillars of Hercules. Although the seaport city is bordered by Morocco, it is a part of Spain's Ca diz Province.

Its sister enclave of Melilla lies more than 150 nautical miles east of Ceuta. Located on a cape that extends about 15 miles from the coast, Melilla is a part of the Spanish province of Malaga. Its area is about 4 square miles (10 square kilometers).

Both cities possess fine ports. Ceuta has the bigger one, which is built around a natural harbor, but both ports service much commercial traffic as well as pleasure craft.

Each of the enclaves has about 80,000 residents, with about 80% being Spanish and much of the rest being Moroccan. A small Indian population is also represented. While Spanish is the language of business and government, both Spanish and Moroccan are widely spoken. Many of the residents of the enclaves are bilingual or understand enough of the second language to converse easily. Most of the residents are either Roman Catholics or Muslims, with the breakdown similar to the ethnic groups — most Spanish are Catholics and most Moroccans are Muslim.

The standard of living in the enclaves is quite good. The enclaves are modern and prosperous, and their residents enjoy a fine lifestyle. Health care and education are roughly equivalent to the levels found in Spain.

Ceuta and Melilla: Yesterday and Today

Both enclaves can trace their history to the Phoenicians, who were probably the first people to trade throughout the entire Mediterranean. After the Phoenicians, the cities continued to share a similar history with various powers of the region gaining control. Spain finally took control of Ceuta in 1580 (losing control to the Moors for the years 1694 to 1520), and gained jurisdiction over Melilla in 1497.

Although the enclaves are officially considered a part of Spain, they occupy a rather unique position. In 1995, Spain granted each enclave autonomy in its own internal affairs. Each city is represented in the Spanish Parliament, and while the province to which each belongs is the overseeing governmental body, by far most of the governmental functions of each city is managed by the local administration.

A potential concern for the enclaves is that Morocco wishes to be given control of the enclaves by the Spanish. Should this happen (which is unlikely) it probably won't result in much change in daily life or routines. Most likely the enclaves, due to their Spanish heritage and history, would continue to function in much the same way they do now. After all, even though they are a part of Spain, they operate with much independence. Furthermore, it is unlikely that Morocco would do anything to disturb the commercial success of the enclaves.

The enclaves provide several important potential benefits to investors. While both enclaves provide easy access to Spain and the rest of Europe, they are both prosperous and enjoy an excellent climate. Because it is smaller, has a smaller port, and its location is somewhat off the main shipping lanes of the Mediterranean, Melilla is the quieter and more relaxed of the two enclaves. Ceuta's position at the headland of the Strait makes it a busy port, handling more traffic than most of the ports of Spain, and its proximity to the mainland — only an hour away from Algeciras by ferry — gives people a quick and economical entry to Spain.

Perhaps even more important for many people is Ceuta's duty-free port for entry to Spain. This has resulted in an impressive growth of countless shops that sell countless items, which in turn supports Ceuta's healthy economy.

Benefits of Ceuta's and Melilla's Tax Systems

The tax systems of the enclaves offer important benefits, including:

- A tax rate of one-half that of Spain.

- No value added tax (VAT).

- Residents of the enclaves benefit from Spain's double taxation treaties.

Should you like to find out more about Ceuta and Melilla, contact:

The Embassy of Spain
2375 Pennsylvania Ave., NW
Washington, D.C. 20037
Tel: 202-452-0100, 728-2340
Fax: 202-833-5670

Tourist Office of Spain
666 Fifth Ave., 35th Floor
New York, NY 10103
Tel: 212-265-8822
Fax: 212-265-8864

Tourist Office of Spain
845 North Michigan Ave.
Chicago, IL 60611
Tel: 312-642-1992
Fax: 312-642-9817

Tourist Office of Spain
San Vicente Plaza Bldg.
8383 Wilshire Blvd., Suite 960
Beverly Hills, CA 90211
Tel: 213-658-7188
Fax: 213-658-1061

Tourist Office of Spain
1221 Brickell Ave., Suite 1850
Miami, Fl 33131
Tel: 305-358-1992
Fax: 305-358-8223

Tourist Office of Spain
2 Bloor St., West, 34th Floor
Toronto, Ontario M4W 3E2
Canada
Tel: 416-961-3131
Fax: 416-961-1992

In addition to the above numbers, for information on commercial matters, contact one of the following commercial offices of Spain at:

New York: 212-661-4959
Washington, D.C.: 202-265-8600
Chicago: 312-644-1154
Los Angeles: 213-627-5284
Miami: 305-446-4387

Chile

Chile is a large country located in southwest South America. It shares borders with Peru to the north, Bolivia and Argentina to the east, and on the west meets the Pacific Ocean. Chile is a long, narrow country, extending north and south for about 2,650 miles (4,270 kilometers), its southernmost region covering the end of the continent. The country is less than 110 miles (180 kilometers) wide. Its overall land area, which includes numerous islands and archipelagoes, is about 292,258 miles (756,945 square kilometers).

Chile's most prominent geographic feature is the Andes Mountains, which rise up to 20,000 feet (6,100 meters) and extend along the eastern edge of the country. Lower coastal mountains meet the Pacific. An extensive plateau lies between the two mountain ranges.

Because of Chile's great north to south length and varying topography, Chile's climate is diverse. Areas of high elevation are colder than nearby lowlands, but in general, as one travels southward the climate becomes temperate with mild winters and cool summers. Rainfall also tends to be more plentiful in the south, a contrast to the north, much of which is covered by the Atacama Desert. In the deep south of the country, the temperature becomes cooler and wetter. Near the southern end of the continent strong storms and winds are common, and mountain peaks in this region remain snow-covered throughout the year.

Chile's population of about 13,000,000 has largely descended in whole or part from pre-Spanish Indians. Only about 2% of the people are of unmixed European descent. Close to 90% of the population is Mestizo, while the remainder of Chile's people are Asians or pure Indians. Close to 90% of the people live in the central region between Concepcion and La Serena, and about 40% live in Santiago, the country's capital. More than 6 out of 10 Chileans is younger than 34 years old, resulting in a substantial consumer base. Spanish is the country's official language, but some Indian languages are still spoken in isolated regions. About 80% of the people are Roman Catholic, with most of the rest belonging to Protestant churches. Some Indians still follow traditional religions, but these are a small minority.

The standard of living in Chile is excellent in comparison to many countries of South America. Education is valued, as evidenced by the country's 95% literacy rate, and the country maintains one of the best health care and social welfare systems on the continent. While some remote areas of Chile are, without doubt, primitive by Western norms, the country's urban areas are entirely modern. Santiago, for example, may be favorably compared to the finest cities in the world. The city offers wide streets that lessen congestion, fine hotels and restaurants, and countless activities from shopping to enjoying the workout of a health club. The beach is just an hour and half drive away, and winter skiing may be enjoyed in the mountains of the east. Chile has something to offer to everyone.

In an effort to expand the country's economy Chile's leaders in recent years have undertaken steps to encourage business. The government understands that a strong economy is vital to improving the standard of living in the country and has enacted legislation designed to encourage investment. Many incentives consist of tax reductions.

Chile: Yesterday and Today

Before the Spanish conquest, the land that became Chile was populated by various Indian groups. In 1535, Diego de Almagro led a troop of Spanish Conquistadors into Chile in search of gold. Almagro had participated in the conquest of the Incas a few years earlier, serving as an aide to Francisco Pizarro. Although Almagro found no gold, in 1540, another of Pizarro's aides, Pedro de Valdivia, headed a second expedition into Chile. Valdivia eventually established Santiago and the Spanish began settlement. Unlike many areas of New Spain, in which the Conquistadors found fortunes in gold and silver, the Spanish found little precious metals in Chile and the colony developed slowly. By the turn of the 19th century, the colony's relations with the Spanish crown were strained and Chile gained its independence in 1826.

Chile has a democratic government, based on a constitution that was first written in 1833. Although Chile is socially and political stable today, the road to stability has been a long one for Chile. During its history the nation has been in conflict with its neighbors, as well as suffering the turmoil caused by rival factions in government. Today Chile's people look forward to the future.

Foreign investors clearly feel that Chile's economic future is bright. In recent years, foreign investment has accounted for close to 20% of Chile's GDP, and exports that are a result of foreign investment operations amount to nearly 25% of the country's total. The view of foreign investors remains positive, in part based on the international rating firm Standard and Poors designation of Chile as a country of low risk. It is expected that Chile will continue to be a favorable site for foreign investment both for the short- and long-term.

Chile's competitiveness has been improving steadily over the last several years. According to the World Economic Forum/IMD, Chile ranked 5th among emerging nations, a designation that placed it ahead of South Korea. Not to be overlooked is Chile's enviable geographical position that enables it to serve as a gateway to Latin-American markets, particularly for U.S. and Asian companies.

Most economic observers feel that Chile's future is one of opportunity. Although the Conquistadors might not have found the gold and silver they sought, Chile possesses abundant minerals and natural resources and is one of South America's foremost producers of minerals. The country is thought to own 25% of the world's copper reserves and is the world's largest copper exporter. Chile's export sector is not relegated to only minerals, however. It is a major exporter, with ties to more than 160 countries, and exports manufactured products, forestry products, fishing products, and agricultural products, all of which are major sectors of the nation's economy. In addition, Chile is fast becoming an exporter of services, including: advertising, engineering, design, printing, and film animation. Currently, Chile exports more than 3,500 products from more than 5,500 companies. Yet another major area of economic activity is the upgrading of the country's infrastructure. While the infrastructure is capable of meeting the nation's current needs, the government is looking to the future and modernizing infrastructure so that Chile has every advantage in the global marketplace.

Benefits of Chile's Tax System

The government of Chile has enacted legislation that provides for various benefits to investors, including:

- The establishment of free zones. Businesses operating in the free zones of Iquique and Punta Arenas enjoy several advantages. Goods imported to the free zone and that remain there are not subject to any value added tax (VAT), nor are there charges for custom duties. Furthermore, companies in the free zones are exempt from VAT on sales and services that occur within the free zones.

- Investors or companies that establish commercial enterprises in Chile's designated remote areas are eligible for exemptions on income tax, VAT, and custom duties.

- Investors or companies that establish commercial activities within the forestry sector may be eligible for —

  - a 50% reduction in personal income tax on income derived from commercial forestry activities.

  - an exemption from property taxes for property deemed suitable for forestry.

  - A 75% subsidy of costs related to the planting of forests.

Should you wish to learn more about Chile, contact the following:

ProChile New York
866 United Nations Plaza, Suite 302
New York, NY 10017
Tel: 212-207-3266
Fax: 212-207-3649

Export Promotion Bureau - PROCHILE
Ministry of Foreign Affairs
General Bureau of International Economic Relations
Avenida Libertador Bernardo O'Higgins 1315, 2nd Floor
Santiago
Chile
Tel: 562-696-0034
Fax: 562-696-0639

National Tourism Board of Chile
Av. Providencia 1550
Santiago
Chile
Tel: 562-236-1420
Fax: 562-236-1417

National Chamber of Commerce Chile
Santa Lucia 302, Piso 4
Santiago
Chile
Tel: 562-639-6639/639-7694
Fax: 562-638-0234

Commercial Bureau of the U.S. Embassy in Chile
Av. Andres Bello 2800
Santiago
Chile
Tel: 562-232-2600
Fax: 562-330-3710

AMCHAM-Chile
Chilean-American Chamber of Commerce
Av. Americo Vespucio Sur 80, Piso 9
P.O. Box 82
Santiago 34
Chile
Tel: 562-208-4140
Fax: 562-206-0911

Colombia

Located in the northwestern region of South America where it links two continents, Colombia occupies a prime position. It is the only country on the continent that has coastlines on both the Atlantic and Pacific, giving it land access to the markets of both North and South America, as well as the islands of the Caribbean and the coasts of the Americas, Europe, Asia, and even Australia.

Colombia is a large country with an area of about 440,000 square miles (1,140,000 square kilometers) and varying topography. Perhaps its most dominating physical feature is the Andes Mountains, extending north to south through the central and western parts of the country and covering close to a third of the country's area. Some of the peaks of the mountains reach 19,000 feet (5,800) meters. Separating the mountains are numerous plateaus and valleys. Colombia also has plains, in the northeast, hot lowlands in the east, and great forests in the south.

Because of the size of its area and its varying elevation, Colombia has several climate zones. Much of the highland areas, which include Bogota, the capital, and most of the major cities, have temperate climates, while the coastal lowlands and many of the valleys are tropical. Rainfall varies, too, tending to be heavier along the Pacific and dryer over the eastern mountains.

Colombia has a population of about 36,000,000. Its people are diverse with about 50% being Mestizo. Another 20% are of pure European descent, and the rest of the people are comprised of blacks, Indians, mulattoes, and zambos, whose lineage has descended from black and Indian blood. Over 70% of all Colombians live in cities, with nearly one out of three living in the country's four big cities of Bogota, Medellin, Cali, and Barranquilla. Most of the people are Catholic, and most speak Spanish, the official language. Many linguists believe that Colombians speak an unadulterated form of Spanish, by many accounts the purest Spanish in Latin America. Regional and local languages are also common.

Although Colombia's general standard of living cannot yet match the typical levels of most Western nations, an excellent lifestyle is possible in the major cities, particularly Bogota. Over 90% of the population is literate — an impressive increase over the literacy rate of 40% in 1950. Most importantly, the government is committed to a program of raising the living standards of its people by improving health, education, housing, and infrastructure.

Colombia: Yesterday and Today

Columbus explored the northern Colombian coast in 1502, and Spanish Conquistadors arrived soon thereafter, establishing the first permanent European settlement on the America mainland at Darien in 1510. Within the next fifty years Spanish settlements were established throughout much of Colombia, and Spain exercised control over the colony for nearly the next three hundred years.

Like most of Latin America, by the early 1800s Colombians longed for freedom from Spain. They gained their independence in 1819 and formed a republic in 1821. The new republic suffered through difficult times and continued only until 1831, after which Colombia was thrown into turmoil by rival political groups. Although the country's troubles continued well into the 20th century, recent governments have taken the necessary steps to stabilize the nation, provide the environment for a robust economy, and raise the country's standard of living.

Many investors believe that Colombia is poised for exceptional economic growth. The country possesses impressive mineral wealth, including significant reserves of gold, silver, iron ore, platinum, tin, and uranium. Already Colombia is the world's leading source of emeralds, and it has substantial energy reserves in the form of fossil fuels. In the coming years Colombia is likely to develop into a major supplier of energy.

In an effort to expand Colombia's economy, the nation's leaders have enacted policies designed to encourage trade on a global scale. The program has been largely successful, and Colombia now has strong trade ties with much of Latin America, the U.S., Europe, and Asia. During the 1990s Colombia's real GDP has outdistanced the average of Latin America, and it is likely to continue to do so in the years to come. It is noteworthy that in every year since 1950 Colombia has achieved a positive GDP growth rate. Between 1990 and 1997, the country's GDP has risen at an average annual rate of 4.1%.

Traditionally, agriculture has been the bedrock of the country's economy. While farm products are still important, the government has taken clear steps to enhance the manufacturing sector. Manufactured products are now an important export, along with textiles and chemicals. It is also likely that Colombia will become a major source of energy, especially with its extensive reserves of oil, natural gas, and coal.

Supporting Colombia's international trade are several trade agreements. The G-3 agreement that includes Colombia, Venezuela, and Mexico has reduced tariffs between the three countries and stimulated commerce. The Chilean-Colombia Treaty of Economic Complementarity has resulted in providing free access to 13 million consumers, and Colombia's membership in the Andean Pact has resulted in free access to 60 million consumers in Peru, Venezuela, Ecuador, and Bolivia. Colombia also receives preferential treatment of its goods in both the U.S. and European Union, giving Colombia access to over 800 million more consumers.

Perhaps *Apertura*, which means **"opening"** and describes an economic modernization program enacted in 1990, best demonstrates Colombia's commitment to a strong economic future. The following goals have been accomplished during Apertura:

- There has been an overall liberalization of trade and the opening of markets.

- Incentives to encourage foreign investment have been enacted.

- Reforms in the banking and financial systems have been enacted.

- Reforms have been enacted in labor laws.

- Foreign exchange has been deregulated.

- Tax reform has been achieved.

- A privatization program has been embarked upon.

- Reforms that have resulted in greater independence for the country's central bank have been completed.

Without question Colombia is on a path that will result in continued economic gains. To help ensure an expanding economy, the government offers major incentives, most notably in free trade zones.

Benefits of Colombia's Tax System

The government of Colombia has established several free trade zones throughout the country. Companies that conduct their business from within a free trade zone are eligible for various benefits, including:

- An exemption from income tax on earnings from exported goods and services. This is a significant exemption, because the overall general tax rate is 30%.

- An exemption from income and complementary taxes for the developers and operators of free trade zones.

- An exemption from income and remittance taxes on payments and transfers overseas. Note that such payments and transfers must cover interest and technical services.

- An exemption from import duties on raw materials, machinery, equipment, and parts that originate overseas and are required by industrial users of free trade zones.

In addition to the above, companies that operate in Colombian free zones may be entitled to the following incentives:

- Freedom to remit profits abroad and repatriate capital.

- The materials purchased by an industrial user from within an area of Colombia outside a free zone are considered to be exports for the domestic supplier. Consequently, the domestic supplier is eligible to receive any available incentives for exporting.

- Since industrial users are permitted to sell their products within Colombia, the sales of such products are considered to be imports.

- Foreign investors who operate a company within a free trade zone are entitled to access all the markets and commercial treaties that Colombia has signed.

- Companies that operate from within a free zone are allowed to use sources of credit in Colombia as well as sources of foreign credit.

Should you wish to find out more information about Colombia, contact the following:

The Colombian Government Trade Bureau
1701 Pennsylvania Ave., NW
Washington, D.C. 20006
Tel: 202-887-9000
Fax: 202-223-0526

The Ministry of Economic Development
Cr. 13 #28-01, 5th Floor
Bogota
Colombia
Tel: +57-1-3200077
Fax: +57-1-2874737

The Ministry of Foreign Relations
Calle 10 #5-51
Bogota
Colombia
Tel: +57-1-3429967
Fax: +57-1-3416777

Information about passports —
Calle 100 #17 A-25
Bogota
Colombia
Tel: +57-1-6107574

Information about visas and immigration —
Calle 98 #17 A-34
Bogota
Colombia
Tel: +57-1-6106345
Fax: +57-1-2575784

Costa Rica

As one of the most stable and democratic countries of Central America, Costa Rica has become a popular destination for businesses and individuals who are seeking a new country in which they can prosper economically. A country about the size of West Virginia, Costa Rica is known for its unsurpassed natural beauty, its hard-working middle class, and its opportunities for investors.

Although it has an area of only 19,730 square miles (about 51,000 square kilometers), Costa Rica has a varying topography of coastal lowlands, an interior plateau, and lusty mountains that rise upwards in some places to 12,000 feet (about 3,750 meters). While climate varies with elevation, much of the country enjoys a tropical climate with a dry season that lasts from December to April and a rainy season from May to November. Temperatures range from an average 68 degrees F (*20 degrees C*) in the mountain valleys to an average of 79 degrees F (*26 degrees C*) in the lowlands along the coasts.

Costa Rica has a population of about 3.5 million, with persons of white and Mestizo descent comprising about 96% of the country's residents, and blacks, Indians, and Chinese accounting for the rest. Spanish is the official language of the country, however, English is common in many of the cities, particularly in and around Puerto Limon. Most Costa Ricans are Catholics.

The standard of living in Costa Rica is one of the highest in Latin America. The literacy rate is 95%, and health care is excellent, though the quality is somewhat reduced in outlying areas. Costa Rica offers numerous activities to augment the country's fine lifestyle. Recreational pursuits include such diverse activities as swimming, surfing, fishing, golf, hiking, kayaking, and scuba diving. Fine restaurants, nightclubs, and shopping are popular in the cities. Sightseeing, especially to observe the wondrous natural scenery, is also a popular activity. Indeed, Costa Rica is considered by many travelers to be one of the most beautiful countries in the world, containing great forests, dry plains, tropical lowlands, and rugged mountains, some of which are home to enormous volcanoes. Although it is a small country, it is estimated that Costa Rica contains about 5% of the world's biodiversity.

Costa Rica: Yesterday and Today

The Spanish arrived early during the period of exploration in 1502 and soon established settlements. Costa Rica remained a Spanish colony until 1821, the year it gained its independence. The former colony was a member of the Central American Federation, a loosely organized entity based on the federal system of the United States, but seceded in 1838. (The federation formally dissolved soon thereafter, resulting in its members becoming independent states.) Since then, except for a civil war that began in 1948 and ended in 1949, Costa Rica has been one of the most stable countries in Latin America. Costa Ricans take pride in their democracy and heritage.

Aware that a strong economy is vital to continued improvement in the standard of living, the Costa Rican government has enacted policies aimed at supporting the nation's trade. Steps have been taken to decrease the nation's fiscal deficit, reduce inflation, increase domestic savings, and improve the general efficiency of government. Several sectors are important to the country's economy, including tourism, agriculture — especially coffee and bananas for export — food processing, textiles, fertilizers, furniture, and cement. The country's infrastructure is generally considered to be modern and solid.

Benefits of Costa Rica's Tax System

While Costa Rica cannot be considered a major tax haven, the country does offer some important tax benefits:

- There is no tax on foreign-source income.

- The rates for payment of income tax in Costa Rica are lower than the rates in most developed countries.

Should you be interested in learning more about Costa Rica, contact the following:

U.S. Embassy (in San Jose, Costa Rica)
APO AA 34020
Tel: 506-220-3939
Fax: 506-220-2305

Costa Rican Consulate
80 Wall St., Suite 1117
New York, NY 10005
Tel: 212-425-2620
Fax: 212-785-6818

Costa Rican Consulate
2112 "S" St., NW
Washington, D.C. 20008
Tel: 202-328-6628
Fax: 202-265-4795

Costa Rican Consulate
185 North Wabash Ave., Suite 1123
Chicago, IL 60601
Tel: 312-263-2772
Fax: 312-263-5807

Costa Rican Consulate
1870 The Exchange, Suite 100
Atlanta, GA 30339
Tel: 770-951-7025
Fax: 770-951-7073

Costa Rican Consulate
1600 NW Le Juene Rd., Suite 102
Miami, FL 33126
Tel: 305-871-7487 or 305-871-7485
Fax: 305-871-0860

Costa Rican Consulate
3356 So. Xenia St.
Denver, CO 80231-4542
Tel: 303-696-8211
Fax: 303-696-1110

Costa Rica Consulate
2901 Wilcrest, Suite 275
Houston, TX 77042
Tel: 713-266-0484
Fax: 713-266-1527

Costa Rican Consulate
1605 West Olympic Blvd., Suite 400
Los Angeles, CA 90015
Tel: 213-380-7915
Fax: 213-380-5639

Costa Rican Investment and Trade Development Board
CINDE Building
La Uruca, San Jose
Costa Rica
Tel: 506-220-0036 or 506-220-0366 or 506-220-4755
Fax: 506-220-4754 or 506-220-4750 or 506-220-4752

Costa Rican Investment and Trade Development Board
CINDE/USA
90 West St., Suite 614
New York, NY 10006
Tel: 212-964-1774
Fax: 212-964-1969

Cyprus

Located in the Mediterranean Sea south of Turkey, Cyprus is an island that offers significant opportunities to investors. Cyprus is a small island with an area of 3,572 square miles (about 9,250 square kilometers), and is a bit smaller than Connecticut. The island's geography features an interior fertile plain between two mountain ranges that extend west to east. The highest point on the island is Olympus at about 6,440 feet (1,952 meters).

Cyprus possesses a temperate, Mediterranean climate with hot, dry summers and cool, wet winters with little extremes in weather. The island's average annual rainfall is about 20 inches (50 centimeters).

The population of the island is about 750,000. Greeks account for about 78% of the residents, Turks comprise 18%, and various groups make up the rest. The greatest majority of Greeks live in what is referred to as the Greek area of the country, and the greatest majority of Turks live in the Turkish section. As would be expected, the country is divided religiously according to ethnicity — most Greeks are Greek Orthodox, while most Turks are Muslim. Other religions on the island include Roman Catholics, Jews, and other minority groups. Three principal languages are spoken on the island: Greek, Turkish, and English.

In the past, Cyprus had been considered to be a "developing" country. That designation changed in 1991 when the World Bank removed the island from its developing country list. Today Cyprus has an acceptable standard of living with a vibrant middle class. The country's literacy rate is 94%, and its level of health care is considered to be good, particularly in the cities.

Cyprus is a republic, the framework of its government expressed in a constitution written in 1960. The head of the government is the president.

Cyprus: Yesterday and Today

Throughout its history, which goes back deeply into prehistoric times, Cyprus has been occupied by various seafaring peoples. Of those who left records of their occupation, the Egyptians, Greeks, Persians, Romans, British, Venetians, and Turks controlled the island, in some cases for centuries. Eventually the British assumed control from the Turks, maintaining administrative duties until 1960 when independence was granted.

Although Greeks and Turks have had their differences on the island, and the island has suffered through times of conflict, today most of Cyprus's citizens prefer to take advantage of the island's growing prosperity. In recent years, the government has focused its efforts on attracting offshore companies as a way to stimulate economic growth. Without question, Cyprus offers offshore companies many significant advantages. Companies on the island enjoy a high-quality, modern infrastructure, low operating costs, and a well-educated workforce. Moreover, business and corporate laws and procedures are modeled after the British system. To further enhance Cyprus as an offshore site, the government provides several noteworthy incentives.

Benefits of Cyprus's Tax System

Cyprus's tax laws are clearly designed to help investors reduce their taxes through the establishment of an offshore company, partnership, or trust. The following incentives are available:

- For offshore companies, the tax rates in Cyprus are 4.25%.

- For partnerships, no tax is required.

- For trusts, no tax is required.

- For branches, when management and control is abroad, no tax is required.

- Limited companies enjoy a tax rate of 10% of normal rates, which may result in an actual rate of 4.25%.

- Dividends derived from offshore companies are not subject to additional taxes, either in regard to the recipient or the company.

- Tax is not required of an offshore company on gains from the sale of real estate that is not located in Cyprus.

- Estate duties are not required on the passing of shares (in the case of death) of an offshore company held by shareholders not domiciled in Cyprus.

The Central Bank of Cyprus provides assistance in the establishment of an offshore company in Cyprus. Contact the bank at:

Central Bank of Cyprus
P.O. Box 5529
Nicosia
Cyprus
Tel: 02-445281
Fax: 02-472012

Should you be interested in finding out more information about Cyprus, contact the following:

The Embassy of Cyprus
2211 R St., NW
Washington, D.C. 20008
Tel: 202-462-5772

The Cyprus Tourist Organization
13 East 40th St.
New York, NY 10016
Tel: 212-683-5280
Fax: 212-683-5282

Cyprus Tourist Office
213 Regent St.
London W1, R8-DA
Great Britain
Tel: 071-734-9822
Fax: 071-287-6534

The Dominican Republic

Centrally located in the West Indies between Puerto Rico, Jamaica, and Cuba, the Dominican Republic is a nation that looks to the future with hope and optimism. Enjoying a strategic position midway in the hemisphere, and also being the closest Caribbean country to Europe, the Dominican Republic is well positioned to prosper in the global economy. To encourage the expansion of business and ensure a growing economy, the country's government has enacted legislation that supports a pro-business climate with several important tax incentives.

Sharing the island of Hispaniola with Haiti, the Dominican Republic is a small nation of about 18,800 square miles (48,734 square kilometers). Several nearby small islands are also a part of the country, most notable of which are Beata and Saona. The island's topography varies from coastal plains to highlands and mountains. Indeed, about 80% of the country is mountainous with the highest elevation of 10,417 feet (3,175 meters) at Pico Duarte.

While the island of Hispaniola enjoys a fine, semi-tropical climate moderated by prevailing easterly winds, climate zones in the Dominican Republic vary according to elevation. Along the coasts the average annual temperature is about 75 degrees F (24 degrees C), with the highland areas considerably cooler. The average annual rainfall is about 60 inches (1,525 millimeters), with most of the rain coming during the wet season from June to November.

The Dominican Republic has a population of about 7 million. About 16% of the people are descended from Europeans, about 11% are black, and the remainder are of mixed races. About 1.6 million people live in Santo Domingo, the nation's capital. Spanish is the major language spoken in the Dominican Republic, but English is common throughout the country. About 90% of the people are Roman Catholic.

In recent years the government of the Dominican Republic has enacted policies designed to improve the country's economy and raise the standard of living of its people. The nation's literacy rate is 74%, but the educational system is improving. Most schools in the cities and large towns provide instruction in English as a second language. Santo Domingo, the capital, is recognized as one of the most enjoyable of all the cities of the Caribbean. It is modern and cosmopolitan and boasts excellent restaurants, clubs, hotels, and entertainment. The Dominican Republic is a country comprised of people who have come from all over the world.

The Dominican Republic: Yesterday and Today

Columbus explored and named the island of Hispaniola during his first voyage to the New World in 1492. The island soon became the site of the first European settlement in the Americas, and Santo Domingo became the first European city. In time, the Spanish, French, Haitians, and English all controlled the island. In 1843, Santo Domingo — which was the name given to the original Spanish part of the island — rebelled against its Haitian rulers and declared its independence. The country has been independent ever since and is governed under a constitution that was adopted in 1966.

From the earliest days of European colonization the economy of the Dominican Republic has centered around agriculture. Sugar cane, coffee, cocoa, and tobacco have always been major crops. The Dominican Republic is one of the world's leading sugar producers, with much of its crop being exported to the U.S. While agricultural products remain important today, the government has adopted a program to diversify the country's economic base by promoting tourism, strengthening the service sector, and supporting manufacturing. During the last ten years the country's economy has undergone significant growth, and during this period has grown faster than most of the economies of the Caribbean. The country has some of the finest hotels in the region and caters to nearly 2 million tourists each year. Its infrastructure has been improved and is considered to be modern and of high quality, and its financial system is one of the most solid in the Caribbean.

Along with benefiting from its location that has resulted in the country becoming a centralized shipping hub, the Dominican Republic enjoys several trade agreements that promote its products. Following are the most significant:

- The Caribbean Basin Initiative results in duty-free entry for products.

- The CBI-NAFTA parity bill ensures that exports of the Dominican Republic enjoy the preferential tariff and quota treatment given to Mexico and Canada under the North American Free Trade Agreement.

- The 806/807 U.S. tariff schedule provides reduced duties for U.S. origin products assembled or processed outside of the U.S. This benefits the textile industry of the Dominican Republic.

- The Lome IV Accorde provides duty-free access of many Dominican Republic products to the European Economic Union (EEU).

In its continuing efforts to expand the country's economy, the government of the Dominican Republic offers various incentives for companies and individuals who wish to invest in the nation. Many of these incentives have the potential to lead to substantial tax savings.

Benefits of the Dominican Republic's Tax System

Free trade zones in the Dominican Republic offer investors excellent incentives. Close to 30 free zone sites are in operation in the country, with several more under construction. Free trade zones in the Dominican Republic enjoy special tax and customs advantages. The zones are open to foreign entities, and already some 400 companies from the U.S., Canada, Europe, and Asia are operating in the zones. Following are some of the most important benefits for companies conducting their business from a Dominican Republic free trade zone:

- An exemption from payments for taxes from 15 to 20 years.

- An exemption from import duties for goods and materials needed for producing export products.

- The freedom to repatriate profits obtained in the zones.

- The option to sell a part of production operations in the local market.

In addition, other incentives may be available, including:

- A free trade zone's operators generally are willing to build industrial units according to a company's needs.

- Joint venture projects are often possible.

- In-house educational programs are often provided.

- Support is given for access to markets in the U.S. and EEU.

- Companies may qualify for special tax incentives (in addition to those mentioned above) from the Dominican Republic.

The government of the Dominican Republic is aware of the importance of a strong economy. To realize that goal, the leadership of the country has worked hard to provide a pro-business, pro-investor environment.

Should you wish to find out more information about the Dominican Republic, contact the following:

The Ministry of Tourism
Av. Mexico Corner 30 de Marzo
Santo Domingo
Dominican Republic
Tel: 809-221-4660
Fax: 809-682-3806

The Dominican Republic Ministry of Tourism
1501 Broadway, Suite 410
New York, NY 10036
Tel: 212-575-4966 or toll free 1-888-374-6361
Fax: 212-575-5448

The Dominican Republic Ministry of Tourism
561 West Diversey Pkwy, Suite 214
Chicago, IL 60614-1643
Tel: 773-529-1336/37 or toll free 1-800-303-1336
Fax: 773-529-1338

The Dominican Republic Ministry of Tourism
2355 Salzedo St., Suite 307
Coral Gables, FL 33134
Tel: 305-444-4592 or toll free 1-818-358-9594
Fax: 305-444-4845

The Dominican Republic Ministry of Tourism
Unit 50 Market Square
Toronto, Ontario
Canada M5E 1T3
Tel: 416-361-2126/27 or toll free 1-888-494-5050
Fax: 416-361-2130

The Dominican Republic Ministry of Tourism
2980 Rue Crescent
Montreal, Quebec
Canada H3G 2B8
Tel: 514-499-1918 or toll free 1-800-563-1611
Fax: 514-499-1393

The Dominican Association of Industrial Free Zones
Gustavo Mejia Ricart 72
Santo Domingo
Dominican Republic
Tel: 809-566-0437
Fax: 809-566-0570

The Central Bank of the Dominican Republic
Ave. Pedro H. Urena
Santo Domingo
Dominican Republic
Tel: 809-221-9111
Fax: 809-686-7488

Dubai

The United Arab Emirates, comprised of seven autonomous states, are located along the southern coast of the Persian Gulf. Of the seven states Dubai offers individuals and companies opportunities for investment as well as the potential for tax reduction. The most important advantages Dubai offers are found in the Jebel Ali Free Zone, which many investors and economists consider to provide some of the best incentives of free zones anywhere in the world.

The land of Dubai, much like that of the other states of the United Arab Emirates, is generally barren and flat with much of its area covered by desert. Dubai's climate is subtropical and arid, with the state receiving only a few inches of rainfall per year. Hot summers with high humidity and pleasant, mild winters are the norm.

About 530,000 people live in Dubai. While most are of Arabic descent, a large percentage is comprised of foreigners who work in the state, taking advantage of the region's robust employment opportunities. Foreign workers come from many countries, including other Arab states, Iran, Europe, and India. Most foreigners live in the cities. The official language of Dubai is Arabic, however, English is common and both Arabic and English are used in business. Other languages are also spoken in the state, with Farsi and Urdu the most common after Arabic and English.

The standard of living in Dubai is excellent. Although the literacy rate is 70%, only people living in isolated areas away from the cities tend to lack education. In the cities and business world the quality of education is high. Because of the large number of foreigners living in the state, numerous private schools have been established to meet the needs of foreign students. The system of health care, like the general standard of living, is of high quality. Dubai's health care professionals are well trained, and the state has modern hospitals and clinics.

It is difficult to become bored in Dubai. Countless recreational activities are available, including: soccer, sailing, swimming, water-skiing, scuba diving, gold, tennis, horse and camel racing, and even car rallying. Because of a climate highlighted by abundant sunshine and warm temperatures, water sports are enjoyed throughout the year. Cities have fine restaurants, hotels, and clubs. Shopping is always an enjoyable experience in the many shops where countless items may be found.

Dubai: Yesterday and Today

Dubai has been a commercial center throughout history, primarily as a stopover for ships and caravans traveling between cities of the West, Far East, and Africa. For centuries, trade was the lifeblood of Dubai, but that changed in 1966 when oil was discovered. Within a decade oil brought wealth to the emirate, enabling its leaders to wisely invest in the state's infrastructure and well-being.

Unlike the leaders of many oil-rich states, the leaders of Dubai realize that the prosperity that comes with oil will not last forever. Once oil reserves are depleted — which is estimated to occur in about 30 years at present rates of consumption — the emirate will need a new foundation for its economy. Rather than wait to develop that foundation once the oil is gone, the state's leaders have undertaken steps to diversify Dubai's economy now. Dubai has used the profits of its oil to build a modern infrastructure, including the Ali Port, and establish the Jebel Ali Free Zone, transforming itself into a major regional industrial and trade site.

In addition, Dubai has adopted an economic policy that clearly provides for a business climate. Consider the following highlights regarding Dubai's economic system:

- Free enterprise and open markets.

- No foreign exchange controls.

- No trade barriers or restrictions on imports.

- Fully modern infrastructure.

- Minimal bureaucracy.

- Encouragement of foreign investors.

- 100% foreign ownership permitted in the Jebel Ali Free Zone.

- Competitive costs for labor.

- Sophisticated financial system.

No less significant is Dubai's position as a takeoff point to the Gulf region's enormous markets. Without question, Dubai is well positioned for continued economic success.

The Benefits of Dubai's Tax System

Dubai's tax incentives center around the Jebel Ali Free Zone, which was created in 1985. The free zone offers facilities that will satisfy the needs of just about any business or industrial operation, including production, warehousing, and shipping. Linked to the free zone is the Jebel Ali harbor, which is the largest manmade — and perhaps the most advanced — harbor in the world. The Jebel Ali Free Zone offers considerable benefits, including:

- No corporate taxes for at least 15 years. The initial 15 year period is renewable for an additional 15 years, as pledged by the government of Dubai.

- No personal taxes for at least 15 years. The initial 15 year period is renewable for an additional 15 years, as pledged by the government of Dubai.

- No import or export duties payable within the free zone.

- No restrictions of currency in the free zone.

To find out more information about Dubai, contact the following:

Dubai Commerce and Tourism Promotion Board
8 Penn Center, 19th Floor
Philadelphia, PA 19103
Tel: 215-751-9750
Fax: 215-751-9551

Dubai Commerce and Tourism Promotion Board
P.O. Box 594
Dubai
United Arab Emirates
Tel: 971-4-511600
Fax: 971-4-511711

Ecuador

Located in northwestern South America, Ecuador is the smallest of what are known as the Andean countries. Despite having an area of 109,480 square miles (283,560 square kilometers) — a little smaller than Nevada — the country has varying topography. A coastal plain, central highlands, eastern jungle, great mountains, and the Galapagos Islands provide Ecuador with a diverse geography that few other countries, even those that are much bigger, can match. Ecuador's mountains, for example, are impressive with Cotopaxi, the tallest, rising up to 19,347 feet (5,897 meters). Cotopaxi is also the highest active volcano in the world.

Because of its varying elevation, and the fact that it straddles the equator, Ecuador, despite its size, has several climate zones. Coastal areas are hot and humid, with jungle lowlands approaching 100 degrees F (38 degrees C) throughout the year, while in some of the higher mountains temperatures may average a cool 45 degrees F (7 degrees C). Between these highs and lows, average temperatures decrease as elevation increases. The jungle lowlands also tend to be the wettest areas of the country, receiving up to 80 inches (200 centimeters) of rain annually. Most other regions of Ecuador alternate between wet and dry seasons.

About 11.5 million people live in Ecuador. Most, about 55%, are Mestizos. The population is also comprised of Indians, 25%, Spanish, 10%, and blacks, 10%. Spanish is the country's official language, however, various Indian dialects are spoken. Most Ecuadorians are Roman Catholic.

The standard of living in Ecuador's major cities is quite good, although conditions decline as one moves into outlying areas. This is particularly true of health care and education. While the overall literacy rate of the country is about 90%, many people in rural areas have what approximates only to an elementary school education.

Although the country's infrastructure in and around major cities is adequate, its quality deteriorates rapidly as one travels to outlying regions. The overall telecommunications system needs to be modernized, ports and airports generally are outdated, and electric power must be expanded. Only the country's major highways and city streets are paved, and many isolated areas have no roads at all. Aware that an inadequate infrastructure undermines economic development the nation's government has taken steps for improvement, but progress has been somewhat slow.

Despite the country's seeming disadvantages, many travelers consider Ecuador to be a land of wondrous natural scenery. Towering volcanoes, Amazon rainforest, marvelous coasts, and the stark beauty of the Galapagos Islands draw visitors from around the world. Recreations are many and varied. Swimming, watersports, scuba diving, hiking, mountain climbing, exploring historic sites, and, of course, dining, dancing, and shopping in Quito, the capital, provide plenty of activities. Quito is a beautiful city that blends buildings from the days of the colonists with modern architecture. On a site near the equator, but nearly two miles high in a valley flanked by mountains, Quito's residents enjoy a climate that is springlike year-round. The view from virtually any vantage point offers majestic snowcapped volcanoes in the distance.

Ecuador: Yesterday and Today

Ecuador has a long history. Prehistoric people lived in the region as early as 12,000 B.C., and it is likely that Polynesians, traversing the Pacific in long dugout canoes, reached the coast soon thereafter. The Incas, the people most associated with Ecuador before the arrival of the Spanish, did not push into the area until the mid 1400s. From the time of their arrival, the Incas controlled the land of Ecuador until the Spanish, led by Pizarro, conquered them in 1532. For the next 300 years, Spain controlled the colony of Ecuador, eventually losing the colony to the liberating forces of Simon Bolivar. Ecuador gained independence in 1830.

Ecuador's history from that time has had periods of calm and turbulence, arising from internal strife as well as from disputes with its neighbors. The last several years, however, have been a time of peace and stability, and Ecuador has developed, in the opinions of many political observers, to be one of the most stable in Latin America. Ecuador is a republic, based on a constitution of 1979 with powers divided between an executive, legislative, and judicial branch.

Ecuador's economy is based primarily on oil and agricultural products. Its oil reserves are considered to be substantial, and it is likely that petroleum will be a major sector of the country's economy for many years. It is notable that Ecuador also possesses mineral wealth, principally in the form of copper, iron, lead, silver, and sulfur. Many of the country's isolated and remote regions have not been fully explored and are thought to contain even more mineral deposits. Agricultural products include bananas, the country's most important export, coffee, rice, and sugar.

Ecuador's government has identified the promotion of local industry, the increase of exports, and an expansion of employment opportunities as the focal points of its economic policy. The government encourages foreign investment and treats foreign and domestic investors equally. Thus, foreign investors are eligible for any tax exemptions, deductions, and discounts that are available to domestic investors.

The cost of living in Ecuador is most appealing. Travelers from the United States, Canada, and Western Europe are often surprised at the low costs for shelter, food, products, and services in Ecuador. A meal in a good restaurant, for example, may cost an equivalent of only a few U.S. dollars.

The Benefits of Ecuador's Tax System

Features of Ecuador's tax laws favor individuals who receive income from outside of the country. Both citizens of Ecuador and foreign nationals are taxed on income derived from economic activities in Ecuador only. Individual taxpayers may benefit from several provisions of the tax code, including:

- Individuals are not required to pay tax on foreign- source income. This pertains to all income earned abroad from any non-Ecuadorian activity, including — but not limited to — interest income, dividends, pensions.

- Ecuador has no provincial, county, or municipal taxes.

- Taxes on inheritance, gifts, and donations apply only on assets located in Ecuador.

- The tax rate for capital gains is 8%.

- Ecuador's basic income tax rates are relatively modest compared to the rates of other countries.

In Ecuador, for example, branches of foreign companies as well as local businesses pay a tax rate of only 25%.

- In the year 2000 Ecuador adopted the U.S. dollar as its currency.

- Foreign investors are able to participate in the Andean Common Market without restriction.

When one considers these tax provisions in the light of the low cost of living in Ecuador, it becomes clear that Ecuador's benefits extend beyond mere taxation.

If you are interested in finding out more information about Ecuador, contact the following:

Embassy of Ecuador
2535 15th St., NW
Washington, D.C. 20009
Tel: 202-234-7200
Fax: 202-667-3482

Consulate of Ecuador
800 Second Ave., Suite 601
New York, NY 10017
Tel: 212-808-0170 or 212-808-0171
Fax: 212-808-0188

Consulate of Ecuador
B.I.V. Tower
1101 Brickelle Ave., Suite M-102
Miami, FL 33131
Tel: 305-539-8214/15
Fax: 305-539-8313

Consulate of Ecuador
500 North Michigan Ave., Suite 1510
Chicago, IL 60611
Tel: 312-329-0266
Fax: 312-329-0359

Consulate of Ecuador
548 South Spring St., Suite 602
Los Angeles, CA 90013
Tel: 213-628-3014 or 213-628-3016
Fax: 213-689-8418

Consulate of Ecuador
151 Bloor St., West, Suite 470
Toronto, Ontario M5S 1S4
Canada
Tel: 416-968-2077
Fax: 416-968-3348

Central Bank of Ecuador
Av. 10 de Agosto y Briceno
Quito
Ecuador
Tel: (2)515-421/518-880

Greece

The Republic of Greece is located at the southernmost part of the Balkan Peninsula. The republic also includes many small islands, which comprise about one-fifth of its total area of 50,944 square miles (131,944 square kilometers).

A land of diverse topography and great beauty, Greece's shores with their numerous bays and inlets meet the Aegean Sea, the Ionian Sea, and the Mediterranean Sea. Plains, valleys, and rugged mountains make up the land. Greece also contains Mount Olympus, the ancient home of the gods in Greek mythology, which rises above the land around it to 9,770 feet (2,917 meters).

Greece's temperate climate is best described as having hot, dry summers and mild, wet winters. The average annual temperature in Athens, the capital, is about 63 degrees F (17 degrees C). In the lowlands summers are typically hot and dry with July high temperatures reaching 99 degrees F (37.2 degrees C). Temperatures are cooler in the mountains. Rainfall varies, with the west coast usually being wetter than the rest of the country.

Slightly more than 10.5 million people live in Greece. About 98% of the population are ethnic Greeks with minorities of Turks, Albanians, Macedonian Slavs, Armenians, and Bulgarians making up the rest. Most people are members of the Greek Orthodox church. Muslims are the next largest religious group, its members comprising just a little over 1% of the population. Although Greek is the country's official language, English and French are also spoken. The literacy rate of Greece is 98%.

While the standard of living in Greece is not equal to that of the most advanced countries of the world, it is quite good. This is particularly true of the major cities where an excellent standard of living is possible. Health care, for example, in the major cities is good. Residents of athens enjoy all the benefits of a major city anywhere in the world.

Greece: Yesterday and Today

Most people are familiar with Greece's history through its mythology which they studied in school. The history of the country, however, extends well back into the period when the earliest seafarers of the Mediterranean sailed in exploration and trade. The many islands and natural harbors along Greece's coast made the land a major center of shipping. A flourishing sea trade along the coasts had already developed by 2000 B.C. Traders and merchants brought with them ideas, as well goods, and it is likely that the early civilization that arose in Greece was in part a result of contact with far-off peoples.

The history of ancient Greece is long and interesting. City states whose citizens bequeathed to the world such things as democracy, philosophy, mathematics, science, and architecture arose, only to eventually be ruled by the Romans, French, Spanish, Italian, and Ottomans. Greece did not achieve independence until 1829.

As befitting a land that gave the world democracy, Greece's government is a parliamentary republic. The current constitution was accepted in 1975.

Over the last several years, the econony of Greece has averaged an annual real GDP growth rate of about 2%. Nevertheless, there are reasons to be optimistic about future economic growth. Greece is a member of the EU and benefits from that organization. The tourist sector has been growing in recent years, the industrial sector has expanded, and agriculture, traditionally a strong sector, remains a vital part of the economy. Greece's telecommunications system is modern, and its overall infrastructure is considered to be adequate. The country also has an advanced system of banking.

The Benefits of Greece's Tax System

When one first examines Greece's tax laws, it is easy to decide that the country has indeed little to offer investors in search of ways to reduce their tax burdens. Greece's tax code contains many taxes. Under Law 89 of the Gree code, however, under the title "Establishment in Greece of Foreign Commercial and Industrial Companies," major tax exemptions are detailed. For some investors, the tax savings can be substantial. Consider the following which are applicable to any foreign commercial or industrial company that establishes a reginal office in Greece:

- A 100% exemption from income tax.

- An exemption from income tax on the earnings of foreign personnel who work for the regional office.

- An exemption from all customs duties, import taxes, stamp duties, and luxury taxes on items imported to equip the regional office.

- An exemption from any export-import duties that might otherwise be due on samples of advertising material by the regional office.

- An exemption from tax on any interest received from deposits in Greek banks.

- An exemption from duties that would normally be required on the importatation of items necessary to furnish the home of the reginal office's foreign personnel.

- An exemption from tax on interest received from government bonds.

- An exemption from tax on the conversion of bond or preference shares of corporations.

- An exemption from tax on the replacement of shares of bond certificates.

- An exemption from tax on interest obtained from loans granted by foreign banks or companies to certain Greek entities.

- An exemption from tax for specific operations from a tax on the profits from the sale of securities.

Special exemptions are provided for the following:

- Foreign companies owing vessels under foreign flags, and which are managed or operated by either a Greek or foreign company, and including the offices or branch offices of foreign companies established in Greece, are exempt from paying taxes, duties, levies, or any withholdings.

- Foreign construction companies whose business focuses on projects outside of Greece but who are established in Greece may be exempt from income tax, duties, levies, and withholding regarding income that arises from operations outside of Greece.

Should you be interested in finding out more information about Greece, contact the following:

The Embassy of Greece
2221 Massachusetts Ave., NW
Washington, D.C. 20008
Tel: 202-939-5800
Fax: 202-939-5824

Consulate General of Greece
69 East 79th St.
New York, NY 10021
Tel: 212-988-5500
Fax: 212-734-8492

The Greek National Tourist Organization
645 Fifth Ave.
Olympic Tower
New York, NY 10022
Tel: 212-421-5757
Fax: 212-826-6940

The Greek National Tourist Organization
Amerikis St.
Athens
Greece
Tel: 01-322-3111/9

The Embassy of the United States in Greece
PSC 108, APO AE 09842
Tel: 30-1-721-2951,8401
Fax: 30-1-645-6282

Guam

Of the Micronesian Islands, Guam is the most modern and advanced, offering opportunities for investment that are hard to find elsewhere. Many investors have come to look upon Guam as a gateway to the Orient and its vast markets, a view that is supported by the facts. In recent years Guam's economy has outperformed most economies of the Pacific, and many investors feel that the potential of the island has not yet been realized. Discounting short-term fluctuations in Asian economic activity, it is expected that Guam's markets will grow in relation to the huge markets around the Pacific. Moreover, being a territory of the United States, Guam enjoys both political and social stability.

In an effort to attract investment to the island, the government of Guam has enacted legislation that makes available several incentives. For some investors, Guam can be a place where they can reduce their taxes while increasing their wealth.

With an area of 209 square miles (540 square kilometers), Guam is the largest of the Mariana Islands. It is also the southernmost, and occupies an enviable location about 6,000 miles west of Hawaii, 1,500 miles southeast of Tokyo, 1,500 miles east of Manila, and 2,100 miles east-southeast of Hong Kong. The island enjoys a tropical climate with an average annual temperature of about 80 degrees F (27 degrees C).

Slightly over 130,000 people live on Guam, of which close to 20,000 are military personnel (and their dependents) of the United States, stationed on the island which is a major defense post in the Pacific. Much of the rest of the island's population is of mixed Pacific heritage, typically Micronesians who speak Chamorro. Both Chamorro and English are official languages, however, English is the preferred language of government, business, and education.

The standard of living on the island is quite good, similar to living standards found in much of the U.S. Health care is also good and is modeled after the U.S. system. Although Guam lacks the exciting, "island" atmosphere of many of the tropical islands of the Caribbean, it offers a host of watersport activities, restaurants, and hotels along with a delightfully slow pace of life amid a wonderful environment.

As a territory of the U.S., Guam's residents enjoy virtually all of the benefits the U.S. affords its citizens. The government is patterned after the federal system of the U.S., and the island's laws are based on the U.S. legal framework.

Guam: Yesterday and Today

Most historians believe that Ferdinand Magellan discovered Guam in 1521 and claimed the island for Spain. The Spanish, however, did not formally take control of the island until 1565, remaining in possession until 1898 when the island was ceded to the U.S. in accordance of the Treaty of Paris that ended the Spanish-American War. During World War II, the Japanese seized Guam in 1941 only to have the U.S. regain it in 1944 in some of the bloodiest fighting in the Pacific. The people of Guam were granted U.S. citizenship in 1950, and the island has gone on to enjoy peace and stability.

Realizing Guam's strategic position for trade in the Pacific, the island government has embarked on plans to expand and diversify the island's economy. In the past, tourism and governmental expenditures — particularly by the military — were the foundations of the economy. Today, various sectors offer potentially excellent growth: agriculture, aquaculture, construction, financial services, manufacturing, wholesaling, and retailing. Light manufacturing has developed as an especially strong sector, helped greatly by Guam's status as a duty-free port which permits free entry of materials that are imported for the manufacture of specific products on the island. Guam's financial system centers around several banks that offer various services to satisfy the needs of investors and businesses.

Supporting the island's economy is a superior infrastructure, a result of the U.S. military's substantial investment in the island. It should be noted that as the U.S. closes other military bases in the Pacific, Guam's importance as a military center rises, ensuring that the island's infrastructure will be continually modernized. It should also be noted that Guam's commercial port, Apra Harbor, is the largest deep-water port between Hawaii and Asia. Many consider the port to be one of the most efficient seaports in the world.

The Benefits of Guam's Tax System

Through the Guam Economic Development Authority, the government of Guam provides various incentives in an effort to attract investment to the island. Most tax incentives are aimed at companies that are willing to invest in the island, and whose operations are likely to create employment for island residents and expand the island's industrial base. Companies that meet the necessary criteria may be eligible for the following tax incentives:

- An income tax rebate of 75% for a period of up to 20 years.

- A rebate of 75% on corporate dividend taxes for a period of up to 5 years.

- An abatement of 100% on real property taxes for a period of up to 10 years.

- An abatement on gross receipts taxes on oil for a period of up to 10 years.

- An abatement on gross receipts taxes on alcoholic beverages made in Guam for a period of up to 10 years.

- Companies that are licensed to carry out their regular business operations on the island are free from paying federal income taxes. They are, however, required to pay a territorial income tax.

- Interest earned by a bank through the operation of an off-shore lending operation in Guam is not considered to be Guam-source income for the purpose of taxation.

  Note that since Guam is a territory of the United States, the tax laws of the U.S. are applicable, except in instances as noted above.

In addition to tax incentives, Guam offers qualififying companies important trade incentives, including the following:

- Duty-free entry for items and materials into U.S. customs Territory for products that are manufactured or assembled in Guam, provided that the products satisfy the requirements that result in Guam being the "country of origin."

- Various trade agreements permit many products manufactured in Guam to be exported to other countries — Japan, Australia, and the nations of the European Common Market — at reduced tariff rates.

If you would like to find out more information about Guam, contact the following:

Guam Economic Development Authority
GITC Building, Suite 911
590 South Marine Drive
Tamuning, GU 96911
Tel: 671-649-4141
Fax: 671-649-4146

Department of Revenue and Taxation
Government of Guam
Building 13-1 Mariner Avenue
Tiyan
Barrigada, GU 96913
Tel: 671-475-5000
Fax: 671-472-2643

Guatemala

Guatemala is a Central American country just south of Mexico. Its western coast gives it access to the Pacific Ocean, while it has access to the Atlantic through the Gulf of Honduras. About the size of Tennessee, Guatemala's area is 42,042 square miles (108,890 square kilometers); its topography includes a narrow western coast and lowlands to the east between which are highlands and mountains. The country is seismically active, most especially in the southern part where several volcanoes highlight the mountains. Volcan Tajumulco is the country's highest point at 13,845 feet (4,220 meters).

While the overall climate of Guatemala is tropical, there are over 300 micro climates, a result of the varying elevations. These micro climates permit the year-round cultivation of numerous agricultural products, making Guatemalan farm produce quite competitive in the winter markets of North America and Europe. Much of the population lives in highland areas, which are where the most comfortable climates and best conditions for agriculture are found. Lowland areas are hot and humid. A rainy season occurs from May to October, and a dry season lasts from November to April.

Guatemala has slightly over 11 million people. Mestizos account for about 56% of the overall population with native Americans comprising the rest. There are few minority groups or pure ethnic Europeans in the country. Spanish is the country's official language, but it is not universally spoken. Only about 60% of the population speaks Spanish with the remaining population speaking any one of several Indian languages, some of which have come down from the original Mayan inhabitants of the region. While Roman Catholicism is the major religion, many Guatemalans are Protestant, and many others, particularly in the outlying areas, still practice religions based on traditional Mayan worship.

The overall standard of living throughout Guatemala does not compare well with advanced or even many other emerging countries. Of the general population, it is estimated that only about 6 out of 10 Guatemalans have access to basic health care, and not much more than half of the country's population is literate. However, conditions are much better in Guatemala City, the capital. Here a comfortable lifestyle is the norm for business people, professionals, and investors. To improve the conditions of its people, the government of Guatemala in recent years has initiated various programs designed to encourage investment and thereby improve the nation's economy. These policies contain significant tax incentives for investors.

Guatemala: Yesterday and Today

When the Spanish arrived in Guatemala, the great Mayan civilization that had flourished in Central America had long been in decline. It was therefore relatively easy for the Spanish to seize the land and establish a colony, which Spain controlled from 1524 to 1821. Upon gaining independence, for a short time Guatemala became a part of Mexico, after which it became a member of the United States of Central America, finally becoming a republic in 1839. The evolution to a full, stable democracy has been a long, hard one, however, as the nation has experienced rule under several dictatorships. Within the last several years, Guatemala seems to have finally established itself as a stable republic.

In the past, agricultural has been the foundation of Guatemala's economy, and farming and farm products remain the most important sector of the economy today. Agriculture accounts for about a quarter of the country's GDP, is responsible for about 65% of the country's exports, and employs nearly 60% of the workforce. Several cash crops are cultivated with sugarcane, coffee, bananas, corn, and beans being the most common. In recent years, beef has become another vital export. Despite the government's efforts to improve the country's manufacturing sector, manufacturing still accounts for only about 20% of the GDP. Moreover, most factories are small, and manufacturing employs only about 14% of Guatemala's workers.

Aside from Guatemala City and other major towns, much of the infrastructure throughout the country needs improvement. The financial system, too, centers around the capital.

Although there are clear weaknesses in Guatemala's overall economic environment, the country has vast potential which many investors have noticed. The country's geographic location positions it near the huge markets of the North American Free Trade Agreement that includes Mexico, the United States, and Canada with some 360 million consumers. Guatemala is also a member of the Central American market with an additional 30 million consumers. The country is developing as a tourist site, especially near its beaches, and ecological tourism is growing enterprise. Pro-business policies have resulted in the growth of construction, the improvement of the infrastructure, and the increase in exports. It should be noted that the Guatemalan economy is fueled by the private sector and the government accounts for only 10% of the country's GNP.

The business environment that has emerged in Guatemala during the last few years is quite attractive. Consider the following:

- The country is stable and democratic.

- The business environment is built around free market policies. Compared to most countries, taxes are low. Inflation is low. The currency is stable and the financial system (around the capital) is sophisticated and sound.

- The country offers a competitive labor force.

- Ports are accessible on both the Atlantic and Pacific via highway and rail systems.

- Business endures minimal bureaucracy.

- There are no limitations on foreign investment, or foreign ownership by corporations or individuals. There are no restrictions on repatriation of capital.

The Benefits of Guatemala's Tax System

Guatemala offers investors several major tax incentives through free trade zones. Guatemalan tax law defines a free trade zone as an area of land specifically designated as a place in which individuals and companies may manufacture or sell goods for export or re-export, or engage in activities of foreign trade. Several incentives are provided by the country's Free Trade Zone Law for service and manufacturing companies established in a free trade zone, including:

- A full income tax exemption for a 12-year period on income derived from the manufacture or providing of services that originate from the company's operations in the free trade zone.

- A full tax exemption on the imports of equipment, machinery, tools, raw materials, containers, packaging, and other items used by the company in the normal operation of its business.

- An exemption of value added tax on goods transferred between free trade zones in Guatemala.

In addition, for companies located within a free trade zone which engage in commercial activities, the following incentives are applicable:

- An exemption from taxes, duties or import charges on commodities and components that are stored in the free trade zone for their use in commerce and trade.

- A exemption of income tax for a five-year period on income derived from commercial activities that take place within the free trade zone.

- An exemption of value added tax on goods transferred inside and between free trade zones in the country.

The Guatemalan government also offers significant tax incentives in the tourism sector, the purpose of which is to encourage and develop the tourist industry. As contained in the Tourism Law, the following tax incentives are applicable for a ten-year period:

- An exemption from all duties and import taxes on raw materials, construction materials, machinery and materials necessary for the business's operation, including vehicles, ships, electrical appliances, cutlery, furniture and entertainment equipment that is not produced in Guatemala or Central America.

- An exemption from real estate taxes on new construction and the expansion and improvement of existing facilities and structures.

The way the Guatemalan tax service calculates tax obligations can also be of benefit to some investors:

- Income tax, which is calculated from gross income, has several exclusions, including: interest from bonds or titles of the government and its agencies, dividends, including stock dividends, and benefits which have already been taxed in another form in the same period.

In an effort to assist investors FUNDESA, the Guatemalan Development Foundation, has created The Guatemala Business Center

(GBC), which is designed to promote the competitive advantages Guatemala offers to investors and businesses. The GBC offers the following services:

- Personalized attention from business professionals.

- Current and essential information on the business climate in Guatemala, as well as markets.

- Recommendation of specialized professionals in the investor's area of interest.

- Establishment of contact with successful businessmen in Guatemala.

- Establishment of contact with private and public organizations that can provide support to a business.

- The Scheduling of visits to Guatemala.

Should you be interested in finding out more information about Guatemala, contact the following:

The Embassy of Guatemala
2220 R St., NW
Washington, D.C. 20008
Tel: 202-745-4952-4
Fax: 202-745-1908

The Embassy of Guatemala
294 Alberto St., Suite 500
Ottawa, Ontario KIP 636
Canada
Tel: 613-224-4322
Fax: 613-237-0492

Guatemala Business Center
1001 Howard Ave. Plaza Tower, Suite 2504
New Orleans, LA 70113
Tel: 504-558-3750 or 800-794-GUAT
Fax: 504-558-3755

Guatemala Business Center
7231 SW 63rd Ave., Suite 101
South Miami, FL 33143
Tel: 305-666-0066 or 800-741-6133
Fax: 305-666-0570

Guatemalan Development Foundation
Diagonal 6, 10-65 Zona 10
Centro Gerencial Las Margaritas, Torre I, Oficina 402
Guatemala, CA
Tel: 502-332-7952 through 56
Fax: 502-332-7958

Honduras

Sandwiched between Guatemala to the north and Nicaragua to the south, Honduras is a Central American country about the size of Tennessee. Much of its overall area of 43,277 square miles (112,090 square kilometers) is comprised of volcanic mountains and large valleys. Close to 40% of the country is covered with forests that yield hardwoods and softwoods, which provide the foundation of a major lumbering industry. The country enjoys access to both the Pacific and Atlantic oceans.

Lying well within the tropical zone, Honduras possesses numerous climates, a result of its varying elevation which in some areas rises upwards of 9,000 feet (2,800 meters). Along the coasts, average temperatures are generally hot with high humidity, while in the mountains temperatures are markedly cooler with lower humidity. A wet season occurs from June to October, while a dry season is the norm for the remainder of the year. Rainfall tends to be greater along the coasts, in some cases up to 100 inches (254 centimeters) per year.

Of Honduras's 5.6 million people, about 90% are Mestizo with the rest comprised of Indians, blacks, and whites. Honduras has the largest Mestizo population of Latin America. Close to 60% of the overall population lives in rural areas, with the rest living in cities and large towns. Most Hondurans are Roman Catholics, though a small percentage (less than 5%) belong to Protestant groups. While Spanish is the country's official language, English is widely spoken, particularly in Tegucigalpa, the capital. Several Indian tongues are also spoken, however, these are mostly confined to remote areas. The country's literacy rate is about 70%, decreasing as one moves away from the cities and towns.

Just as with education, the standard of living declines as one moves into less populated areas. Health care, for example, is considered to be good in the capital, but is far from adequate for most of the people who live outside of major cities.

Without question, Honduras is one of the poorer countries of Latin America, however, poverty does not affect the entire country. Indeed, a comfortable lifestyle can be had in many places, especially the capital and cities. Comfortable, expansive homes are common in upscale neighborhoods where residents — professionals, business people, and government officials — enjoy a lifestyle comparable to any in North America. Fine restaurants, shopping malls, supermarkets, theaters, a variety of recreational activities, including membership in exclusive country clubs, help to ensure that boredom doesn't occur in Honduras for those with the necessary resources.

Honduras: Yesterday and Today

The Spanish colonized Honduras during the 1500s and retained control until 1821 when the colony gained independence. The new country joined the Central American Federation, but was soon independent once more after the dissolution of the Federation in 1839.

Honduras's history is highlighted by its struggle toward democracy. The country has certainly suffered through long periods of military rule, conflict, and oppression. Since 1989, however, with the election of a civilian government committed to bringing political stability and economic growth to the country, Honduras has begun a new period in which the country has moved forward to bring its people peace and prosperity.

The country today is a stable democracy in which a pro-business climate prevails. Unfortunately, progress has been slow. Despite the government's efforts at expanding the nation's industrial base, Honduras's economy centers around agriculture, which accounts for over 60% of the country's exports and nearly 65% of its jobs. Coffee and bananas are the chief crops. Manufacturing accounts for about 20% of the nation's exports.

Several factors point to excellent potential for the expansion of the Honduran economy. The telecommunications system, especially in and around the capital and other cities, is modern, while the overall infrastructure is quite good. Honduras has several seaports, of which Puerto Cortes, the only deep water port in Central America, is one of the region's most modern. Four international airports serve Tegucigalpa. Honduras's electrical generating capacity is not only capable of providing for the country's needs, but is also able to generate power for export. The country's financial system is rapidly developing and currently includes several major banks that offer a full range of services for both consumers and businesses.

The Benefits of Honduras's Tax System

The major incentives provided in the Honduran tax code are designed around the country's Free Trade Zones and Export Processing Zones (EPZ). For some investors, the advantages offered are substantial.

A good example is the Inhdelva Free Trade Zone. Located about a 15-minute drive from San Pedro Sula, the country's largest industrial city, the Inhdelva Free Trade Zone is also only about 30 minutes from Puerto Cortes Port. The zone itself is operated by Inhdelva, a private concern supervised by the government. For companies operating within the zone, the following incentives are available:

- No federal, state, or local income, sales, or corporate taxes.

- Duty free import of production machinery, equipment necessary to the company's business, parts, raw materials, and supplies.

- Currency conversion without restriction.

- Withdrawal of capital or profit taking without restriction.

- A full exemption from export duties, fees, and controls.

In addition, companies operating from within the zone enjoy the following:

- Duty free commerce of many products shipped to North America under existing programs.

- As noted in the U.S. Caribbean Basin Initiative, many Honduran products may enter the United States duty free.

- Access to low-cost skilled and unskilled labor.

- Access to a wide range of low-cost raw materials.

Like the free trade zones, export processing zones provide several important incentives for factories located within the zone, including:

- An exemption from taxes for as long as the factory remains in the EPZ.

- No restrictions in regards to foreign exchange or the repatriation of capital or profits.

- A guarantee of private ownership and operation.

- Simplified customs' clearances.

If you would like to learn more about Honduras, contact the following:

The Embassy of Honduras
3007 Tilden St., NW
Washington, D.C. 20008
Tel: 202-223-0185, 0187 Economic Section: 202-966-7702
Fax: 202-966-9751

Consulate General of Honduras
80 Wall St., Suite 915
New York, NY 10005
Tel: 212-269-3611

Consulate General of Honduras
1707 N. Burling St.
Chicago, IL 60614
Tel: 312-951-6382
Fax: 312-951-6394

Miami Consulate of Honduras
300 Sevilla Ave., Suite 201
Coral Gables, FL 33134
Tel: 305-447-8927

Honduras-American Chamber of Commerce
Hotel Honduras Maya Ap. Postal 1838
Tegucigalpa
Honduras, C.A.
Tel: 504-32-7043
Fax: 504-32-2031

General Directorate of Export and Investment Promotion
4to. piso. Edificio Salame
Tegucigalpa
Honduras, C.A.
Tel: 504-37-1850
Fax: 504-37-8138

Hong Kong

By the time Hong Kong was reunited with China on July 1, 1997, thousands of its most prominent businessman, professionals, and citizens had already left, certain that as British dependency ended, so too would Hong Kong's prosperity. Today, most of those same people have returned, eager to resume their lives and economic pursuits, convinced now that Hong Kong will remain a successful center for business for many years.

Since its official change in status, Hong Kong is called the Hong Kong Special Administrative Region, usually referred to as Hong Kong SAR. Despite the Chinese takeover, and indeed with Chinese approval, the region has remained committed to its free market economy.

Located in eastern Asia on the South China Sea, Hong Kong consists of a part of the mainland and several islands, comprising an area of only 403 square miles (1,045 square kilometers). Hong Kong's climate is a pleasant one, somewhat cool and humid throughout the winter and warm and wet from spring through summer. Autumns are often mild and sunny, and many residents feel that this is the best time of year in the region. There is not a large degree of temperature contrast throughout the year. The average high temperature in July is 82 degrees F (28 degrees C) while the average low in February is 59 degrees F (15 degrees C).

About 6.3 million people live in Hong Kong. Some 90% are Chinese, with the remainder of the population made up of various minorities from around the world. Close to 90% of the residents belong to major and local religions of Asia, while the other 10% are mostly Christian. The most common languages of Hong Kong are Chinese (Cantonese) and English, which is often used in international business. The literacy rate of the region is 92%.

The standard of living in Hong Kong is one of the highest in the world. Health care is excellent, and a modern infrastructure and high-quality telecommunications system are equal to those of the world's most advanced countries. Unquestionably, Hong Kong offers its residents a life full of pleasures, convenience, and opportunity.

Hong Kong: Yesterday and Today

The British gained control of Hong Kong in the Treaty of Nanking in 1842, which ended the Opium War between China and Great Britain. The Chinese always desired the area's return, finally achieving their goal in an agreement signed with Britain in 1984 which pledged the return of Hong Kong. The British continued to maintain control of Hong Kong until July 1, 1997, when the region was officially turned over to the Chinese.

While under British control, Hong Kong's laws and institutions were based on British common law and political and social systems. China has promised to respect Hong Kong's existing social and economic framework for 50 years, and so far has honored its commitment. This is a logical policy by the Chinese, because it helps to ensure Hong Kong's continued economic success which not only benefits the residents of Hong Kong but the mainland as well. Predictions for the long-term, of course, are difficult to make given the politics of the region, but any changes are likely to be gradual and minimal.

The reasons for this are clear: With GDP per capita at about U.S., $27,500 Hong Kong is an economic powerhouse. Hong Kong's free market system is one of the most open in the world, and the opportunities it offers to investors are considerable.

While Hong Kong provides investors with substantial tax incentives, the region is more than just a tax haven, but a true business haven as well. In most tax havens, the ability to add value to services provided is minimal. Consider the reinvoicing business. Most jurisdictions that are clearly tax havens are home to trading companies that do little more than reinvoicing. A firm in Hong Kong, however, has expanded this concept with the ability to arrange local trade financing, in effect turning Hong Kong into an offshore business center.

The company is ICS Trust Company Limited, which is part of the ICS International group of companies that maintains its headquarters at Hong Kong. Elizabeth L. Thomson, the woman who began this group, describes herself as "a lawyer by profession" and "an entrepreneur by choice." (Thomson has earned two law degrees, and is a member of four international law societies.) Having helped people around the world to start successful new businesses, Thomson's experience and reputation are excellent. She is also well known and respected for helping women entrepreneurs in Hong Kong.

ICS, with a staff of 40 highly qualified individuals, offers services for virtually every facet of a business, including incorporation, financing, management, and even investment of profits. Clients of ICS include multinational companies as well as international investors who are interested in tax shelters and estate planning.

ICS is ideal for the business or investor that wishes to expand into the Asian marketplace. ICS has the contacts that can facilitate any business's setup or expansion in Hong Kong. Drawing upon their extensive banking contacts, ICS professionals can help a business find the best credit facilities for their operation, in many cases, depending upon the client, arranging for either a zero or extremely low margin deposit, thus freeing up capital and collateral that the business may then use to increase sales and achieve greater profits. ICS also works with factories, shipping companies, and freight carriers, and will structure conditions and transactions so that your business will benefit from flexible, low cost facilities.

ICS can even manage a Direct Import Program for you. For example, if you import goods from Asia for sale to large chains, ICS can help you expand your credit facilities and increase your domestic sales. The Direct Import Program can result in a substantial increase in profits by setting up a system whereby customers feel that they are buying "direct." This may be done by:

- Setting up a subsidiary company in Hong Kong.

- Having your buyers open their L/C or orders with this subsidiary.

- Forming liaisons with suppliers that will ensure that goods are produced according to specification. The Direct Import Program achieves success primarily because of two reasons:

- The current trend in the retail industry is for buyers to "buy direct" from Asia. (Maintaining a subsidiary in Hong Kong which receives orders therefore is essential.)

- Major retain chains can usually obtain freight and insurance costs at substantial savings because they are buying in large numbers. Selling FOB in Asia can often lead to a lower selling price for the importer while keeping the same profit.

ICS professionals can set up and manage a subsidiary company for you. They can arrange for all aspects of the establishment of the subsidiary, from obtaining financing to the actual handling of the orders. Customers will view you as an Asian supplier, who maintains a Hong Kong office, and will be satisfied that they are buying direct.

To find out more how ICS can help you and your business or investments, contact:

Mr. Kishore K. Sakhrani, Director
ICS Trust (Asia) Limited
Nine Queen's Road
Suite 605-6, Central
Hong Kong
Tel: +852-2854-4544
Fax: +852-2543-5555

There are many reasons to consider investing in Hong Kong. The Heritage Foundation of the United States has rated Hong Kong as the world's freest economy for the past four years. Hong Kong clearly is pro-business and pro-investment. Consider the following facts about Hong Kong's economy:

- The economy is built on free market principles; the market is open and free to all. There are no restrictions.

- There are no tariffs, quotas or other barriers to trade.

- There are no restrictions on investments.

- There are no foreign exchange controls.

- The trade-to-GDP ratio is 300%.

- The volume of Hong Kong's trade is behind that of only the United States, the EU, and Japan.

The Benefits of Hong Kong's Tax System

Hong Kong's tax system is one of the most pro-business in the world, offering incentives to companies and investors. Some of its most important benefits include:

- Only income derived from Hong Kong is taxable.

- Companies pay only 16% profits tax.

- Individuals pay no more than 15% in salaries tax.

- There is no value added tax.

- There is no sales tax.

- There is no capital gains tax.

- There is no withholding tax on dividends and interest.

- There is no global taxation.

Should you be interested in finding out more information about the investment and tax-reducing possibilities in Hong Kong, contact the following:

Hong Kong Economic and Trade Office
680 Fifth Ave., 22/F
New York, NY 10019
Tel: 212-265-8888
Fax: 212-541-7321

Hong Kong Economic and Trade Office
1520 18th St., NW
Washington, D.C. 20036
Tel: 202-331-8947
Fax: 202-331-8958

Hong Kong Economic and Trade Office
130 Montgomery St.
San Francisco, CA 94104
Tel: 415-835-9300
Fax: 415-421-0646

Hong Kong Economic and Trade Office
174 St. George St.
Toronto, Ontario
Canada M5R 2M7
Tel: 416-924-5544
Fax: 416-924-3599

Hong Kong Trade Development Council
38/F Office Tower, Convention Plaza
1 Harbour Road, Wan Chai
Hong Kong
Tel: 852-2584-4333
Fax: 852-2824-0249

The Republic of Ireland

Through a variety of tax and business incentives, the Republic of Ireland offers investors superb opportunities that can not only enable them to increase their profits but help them reduce their tax burdens as well. Some investors consider Ireland to be one of the best places for investment in the world. (Note that the information that follows pertains to the Republic of Ireland and not Northern Ireland, which remains a part of the United Kingdom.)

With an area of about 27,136 square miles (about 70,280 square kilometers) the Republic of Ireland covers the greater part of the island of Ireland. Northern Ireland comprises the rest of the island's 5,500 square miles (about 10,110 square kilometers).

The land of Ireland consists of an assortment of small mountain ranges and lowlands. While the east coast is relatively flat, the west coast is highlighted by islets, inlets, and steep cliffs. The island's climate is moderated by the warm waters of the Gulf Stream that flow across the North Atlantic. Despite its path of several thousand miles, the Gulf Stream retains enough of its warmth to raise the temperature of Ireland about 25 degrees F (14 degrees C) higher than other lands at similar latitudes. The temperatures of the island have few extremes. Ireland's average summer temperatures range between 57 and 68 degrees F (14 degrees to 20 degrees C), and its average winter temperatures range between 40 and 45 degrees F (7 to 14 degrees C). Rainfall averages about 40 inches per year (100 centimeters). There is no distinctive wet or dry season.

About 3.7 million people live in the Republic of Ireland, with nearly a third of them living in or around Dublin, the capital city. The great majority of modern Irish are descended from the Celts, an ancient people that once stretched across much of Northern Europe. The English are the only significant minority. English and Irish (also known as Gaelic) are the official languages of the country, with English being the most widely spoken. Over 90% of the population are Roman Catholics, while the rest of the people belong to Protestant sects or other religions.

The standard of living in Ireland is high, comparable to the living conditions of other European countries. The Irish literacy rate is 99%, and the quality of the nation's health care is good, again comparable to most of Europe.

Ireland, often noted as the most pollution-free country of Europe, is also considered by many to be one of the most beautiful of the continent, if not the world. Meadows of wild flowers, lush fields, and shady glens are found throughout the island. Along with its natural beauty, Ireland has a fascinating history and culture, offers numerous recreations — from hiking over heather-covered hillsides to hobnobbing in local pubs — and promises a quality of life that will be hard to find anywhere else.

Ireland: Yesterday and Today

About 350 B.C. the Celts came to Ireland from the European continent and quickly subdued the tribes that inhabited the island. The Celts were dominant for the next 1200 years, until Vikings began raiding the Irish coast. The Viking assaults continued for nearly two hundred years, a time during which many Vikings settled along coastal areas and inland rivers, building villages and towns. War between the Vikings and the Celts continued for years. The English also began looking toward the island. As early as 1250, they had gained control of much of Ireland, though they fought periodic wars with the Irish for the next six and a half centuries. In 1921, the Anglo-Irish Treaty freed the counties that would eventually become the Republic of Ireland, though full independence didn't come until 1949. (Because they had a Protestant majority and more closely identified with England, the counties of Northern Ireland preferred to remain a part of the United Kingdom rather than join the Republic.) The government of the Republic of Ireland is modeled after the British government and its laws are based on British common law.

Traditionally, Ireland's economy was based on agriculture. Today, agriculture is still important, but it accounts for only about 20% of the country's GNP. This is a result of policies put in place by the Irish government that were designed to strengthen and diversify the nation's economy. Light industry, tourism, and the financial service sectors have all become important parts of the economy. Of these, perhaps the most successful has been the emergence of the Republic of Ireland as a financial services center, with Dublin becoming a major center for international offshore funds management in Europe.

Ireland's financial services sector is quite sophisticated and offers numerous services in areas such as funds management, international banking, insurance, and asset finance. The country's financial system includes a variety of major banks, investment and funds companies, credits companies, and credit unions, all rigorously supervised by the Central Bank of Ireland.

Unquestionably, in recent years, the Republic of Ireland has developed into one of the best sites for investment opportunity in Europe. Within the last three decades more than a thousand major overseas companies have established operations on the island.

Supporting the country's economy is a fully modern infrastructure. The telecommunications system is of the highest quality, international airports are located at Dublin, Shannon, and Cork and provide Ireland with regular service to major cities worldwide, and the country's roads are well maintained and connect virtually all parts of the nation. Several ports accommodate sea transport.

The Republic of Ireland has enjoyed solid economic growth over the last several years. In an effort to maintain that growth, the government is likely to continue incentives for investors, providing investors and businesses with outstanding opportunities.

The Benefits of the Republic of Ireland's Tax System

The tax code of the Republic of Ireland includes several taxes, including an income tax, however, major incentives provide excellent advantages and can significantly reduce the tax burden. Note the following:

- Foreign income, excluding income from the United Kingdom, is not chargeable for non-domiciled residents, except to the extent that such income is remitted to the Republic of Ireland.

- Nonresidents who receive interest payments from a financial services firm that is located at the Customs House Docks Area in Dublin are not subject to withholding taxes on payments.

- Specific manufacturing companies are eligible for a 10% corporate tax rate on income from the sale of goods manufactured by the company in the state. The rate may apply to both goods which are considered to be manufactured, as well as goods and services that are specifically designated by legislation as qualifying for the benefit.

- Specific manufacturing companies are eligible for a 12.5% rate for trading profits, which will apply from January 1, 2003. (Companies already in operation and which are eligible for the 10% rate will retain that rate until the end of the year 2010.)

- Companies beginning new projects may be eligible after July 22, 1998 for the 10% rate in their specific activities until December 31, 2002, there-after being subject to the 12.5% rate.

- International financial services firms that are located at the Customs House Docks Area in Dublin may be eligible for the 10% rate of corporation tax for trading.

- Certain international financial services companies located in Dublin may be exempted from local property taxes for a period of up to 10 years.

- Certain international financial services companies located in Dublin may enjoy a 100% write-off for expenditures for new equipment during their first year of operation, a 100% write-off for the costs of new facilities in the first year for owners who occupy their sites, and a 54% write-off for new building costs in the first year for lessors.

- Companies granted permission to operate in the Shannon Airport Customs Free Zone are taxed at a rate of 10% through December, 2005.

- In addition, a variety of tax incentives apply in other areas, including:

- An exemption from income tax and corporate taxes on income from commercially managed woodlands.

- Companies that promote and foster business in areas designated as inner city areas in Dublin, Cork, Waterford, Galway, and Limerick may be eligible for various tax incentives.

- The owner(s) of a stallion is exempted from paying tax on income from stallion fees for the servicing of mares in Ireland.

- For those individual investors and companies that invest in a film-making project in Ireland, tax relief is possible.

Should you wish to find out more about what opportunities the Republic of Ireland offers, contact:

The Industrial Development Authority
17th Floor, 345 Park Ave.
New York, NY 10154
Tel: 212-750-4300
Fax: 212-750-7357

The Industrial Development Authority
75 East Wacker Dr., Suite 600
Chicago, IL 60601-3708
Tel: 312-236-0222
Fax: 312-236-3407

The Industrial Development Authority
1620 26th St., Suite 480 South
Santa Monica, CA 90404
Tel: 310-829-0081
Fax: 310-829-1586

The United States Embassy in Ireland
42 Elgin Road, Ballsbridge
Dublin
Ireland
Tel: +353-1-668-8777

The Irish Tourist Board
Baggot Street Bridge
Dublin 8
Ireland
Tel: +353-1-602-4000
Fax: +353-1-602-4000

A special source of help in Ireland.

There is an Irish firm that I am particularly pleased to recommend. Fitzgerald & Associates, one of Ireland's leading accounting, financial and tax consulting firms, is a dynamic, growing firm of registered auditors, business advisers and accountants with offices in Cork and Dublin. The head of the firm, John Fitzgerald, is a law graduate and barrister as well as an accountant.

Apart from the usual accounting and auditing services, they are involved in comprehensive tax planning for both individuals and corporations, in corporate finance services such as advice on funding, financial planning, management buyouts, and the negotiation of Irish government grant assistance. They give advice on mergers and acquisitions and preparation of documents for public securities issues by Irish companies.

They form Irish companies, and can provide the company secretary and other statutorily-required company services.

To discuss specific services with them, please contact:

John Fitzgerald
Fitzgerald & Associates
6 Sullivan's Quay
Cork, Ireland
Telephone: +353 21 963877
Fax: +353 21 310273

Israel

Israel is a small Middle East country. With an area of only 7,992 square miles (about 20,700 square kilometers), it is about the size of New Jersey, but its size, certainly, is not in relation to the headlines it gains in the world's news. In recent years, the headlines have announced progress in peace initiatives more often than the violence brought about by radicals who prefer to keep the region in turmoil and conflict. Perhaps because news about Israel relates in one way or another to the peace process, not much is reported about the investment opportunities — some of which include important tax savings — that are offered by the Israeli government in an effort to enhance the growth and diversification of the country's business and industry.

A land of plains and low hills, Israel meets the Mediterranean Sea on the west and shares borders with Lebanon to the north, Jordan to the east, and Egypt to the southwest. Israel's climate is subtropical, but with major variations depending on location. Average annual temperatures may vary from 40 degrees F (*5 degrees C*) in winter to 95 degrees F (*35 degrees C*) in summer. In the northern part of the country, rainfall averages about 32 inches (80 centimeters) per year, while in the south less than 2 inches (3.5 centimeters) of rain falls in an average year. In most parts of the country, summers tend to be hot and dry while winters are cool and wet.

Israel has a population of about 5 million, with 83% of its people being Jewish and the rest being Arab. Most of the people, of course, adhere to Judaism, with about 14% of the population being Muslim and the rest being Christian. Both Hebrew and Arabic are official languages, but English is spoken throughout much of the country and particularly in the cities.

The standard of living in Israel is high, and its system of health care is comparable to those of advanced nations. The literacy rate among the Jewish population is well over 90%, but it is only about 70% for the Arab population. Despite what one may hear on the evening news about violence in Israel, most of the country is secure and people enjoy a variety of recreations that may be found in any western land.

Israel: Yesterday and Today

Israel's history begins in Biblical times. The land has been the site of conflict for thousands of years and has been controlled by Jews, Babylonians, Persians, Greeks, Romans, Seljuks, Mamluks, Christian Crusaders, and Ottomans. Israel finally gained its independence through a United Nations resolution in 1948. The resolution, which was unacceptable to Arab states, led to several wars between Israel and Arab states that spanned the next forty years. Not until the early 1990s did peace talks begin, and finally, in 1993, a peace agreement was signed between Israel and the Palestine Liberation Organization (PLO). The peace accords are still moving forward today, despite the efforts of radicals to plunge the region back into war.

Israel's government is a parliamentary democracy in which executive power resides with the prime minister and legislative power rests with the parliament. The country's judicial system has two parts: a civil system that addresses cases of a criminal or civil nature, and a religious system that deals with court cases having to do with marriage, divorce, alimony, and wills.

Because of the demands of defense, the government has always played a strong role in the development and maintenance of Israel's infrastructure. Consequently, Israel possesses one of the finest infrastructures in the Middle East. The nation's economy is also diversified, and Israel is in an excellent position to take advantage of the huge markets of the region.

The Benefits of Israel's Tax System

Forced to fund a large defense budget, Israel's tax code includes numerous taxes. However, notable incentives and exemptions are also included, which can prove to be significant for certain individuals and investors. Free trade zones also offer major incentives.

Certain individuals may be exempt in part or whole from income taxes, including:

- New residents in respect of income that is received from abroad during the first seven years of residence.

- Temporary residents in respect of income that is derived from sources abroad, provided the individual has not lived in Israel for more than six months in the year preceding assessment and the individual does not intend to become a permanent resident.

- Nonresidents in respect of interest on specific types of securities and loans.

- Certain dependents of deceased members of fighting services in respect of pensions paid by the government.

- Certain victims of hostile action or Nazi persecution.

- Certain victims who suffer from handicaps.

In addition exemptions are possible for taxes on capital gains that are derived from securities found on the Tel Aviv Stock Exchange.

Hopeful of attracting investment from both domestic and foreign sources, the Israeli government has approved legislation containing several important incentives. To be eligible for such incentives, a company must be designated as an Approved Enterprise. Possible incentives include:

- Reduced tax rates to as low as 10% for a period of 10 years.

- Grants of up to 38% of the cost of fixed assets. If the right to receive such grants is waived, a full tax exemption for up to 10 years may be obtained.

- Accelerated schedules for depreciation of equipment may be permitted.

A company that operates in an Israeli free zone may be entitled to various incentives, including:

- Companies that conduct their business from the Free Port Zones of Eilat, Ashdod, and Haifa are eligible for an exemption from all income taxes for a period of seven years. In addition, they receive a maximum tax rate of 30% after the seven-year period, a tax of 15% of dividends derived from income, and an exemption from property taxes. Some companies may also be exempt from capital gains tax for shareholders.

- Companies that conduct their business from the Eilat Free Trade Zone are exempt from value added tax and receive refunds of up to 20% on the gross wages paid to their employees. In addition, individuals who reside in Eilat may receive tax credits of up to 10% of their taxable income that is obtained from employment or business conducted in the zone.

Should you like to learn more about Israel, contact:

The Israel Government Tourist Office
800 Second Ave.
New York, NY 10017
Tel: 212-499-5650, 5645 or 800-596-1199
Fax: 212-499-5655

The Israel Government Tourist Office
24 King George St.
Jerusalem
Israel
Tel: +972-275-4863

The Minister of Economic Affairs
Embassy of Israel
3514 International Dr., NW
Washington, D.C. 20008
Tel: 202-364-5692
Fax: 202-364-5647

<u>Jordan</u>

Jordan is a small Middle East nation that shares its northern border with Syria, its eastern border with Iraq and Saudi Arabia, its southern border with Saudi Arabia, and its western border with Israel. Having access to the Gulf of Aqaba in the south, Jordan truly is a crossroads of the region.

Jordan is a high, dry land. Slightly smaller than the state of Indiana, the country has an area of 37,738 square miles (97,740 square kilometers), most of which is a plateau that averages between 2,000 and 3,000 feet in elevation (600 to 900 meters). Except for the western part of the country which experiences a wet season from November to April, much of Jordan is arid. While the wettest regions of the country receive only about 26 inches (66 centimeters) of rainfall per year, the eastern part of the country is dry and almost desert-like. Temperatures vary with location, sometimes reaching 120 degrees F (49 degrees C) in the Jordan Valley in the summer, while the temperatures in Amman, the capital city, may be 10 to 20 degrees cooler. Although some parts of the country reach freezing temperatures in the winter, the country's overall average winter temperature is about 45 degrees F (7 degrees C).

About 98% of Jordan's 4.2 million people are Arab, with the remainder being comprised of Circassians and Armenians. Close to 92% of the population are Sunni Muslim and the rest are Christians. The country's official language is Arabic, however, English is understood by the nation's upper classes and professionals and is spoken in many parts of the country, particularly in the international business sector. The importance of English is underscored by the many businesses and road signs that are written in both Arabic and English. The overall literacy rate in Jordan is 86%, with education being greater in the cities and large towns and decreasing in outlying areas.

The standard of living in Jordan is excellent, especially among the upper segments of Jordanian society. Health care is good, most notably around Amman, and the medical profession is well trained. Jordan offers a fully modern lifestyle to its residents and visitors. Shops, stores, and supermarkets offer numerous consumer items, fine restaurants and hotels are located in Amman, and various recreational activities are available.

Recognizing the need to strengthen the country's economy and take advantage of the expanding markets in the Middle East, Jordan's government has enacted a variety of incentives to encourage international businesses to establish operations in the country. There are, unquestionably, superior investment opportunities.

Jordan: Yesterday and Today

Some of the world's first notable civilizations arose in Jordan, and since those times numerous people have controlled this land. Indeed, the Eqyptians, Assyrians, Babylonians, Persians, Romans, Arabs, Ottoman Turks, and British at one time or another ruled Jordan, leaving their mark on the country's history. It was from the British that Jordan (at the time called Transjordan) gained "qualified" independence in 1928, though full independence was not granted until 1946.

After gaining independence, Transjordan ("Trans" was not officially dropped from Jordan's name until 1950 when the country merged with Arab-held Palestine) found itself allied with other Arab states and at war with Israel. For many of the following years, Jordan found its economy greatly undermined by the tensions and conflict in the region.

In recent years, the government and people of Jordan have come to understand that peace is essential for economic expansion and prosperity. To this end, Jordan negotiated a peace treaty with Israel that established diplomatic relations and fostered economic cooperation and security between the two nations.

Since it has chosen peace instead of confrontation and war, Jordan, unlike many of its Arab neighbors, has achieved a large measure of economic, social, and political stability. The country's government is a constitutional monarchy with a bicameral legislature. Although the head of the government is the prime minister, the chief of state is the king who wields considerable power. The country's legal framework is based on Islamic law and French legal codes.

Jordan's government recognizes the need for diversification of the nation's economy. Recent policies that have been enacted reflect the government's objectives to:

- Reassess and redefine the role of the state and enhance the role of the private sector.

- Encourage investment, particularly in the export and production sectors.

- Stabilize the exchange rate of the Dinar, the nation's currency.

- Reduce the level of foreign debt.

- Encourage foreign investment through numerous incentives aimed at specific sectors of the economy.

- Provide incentives for savings.

- Open markets and the flow of trade.

Jordan's economy is built around agriculture and a few major industries. About 20% of the labor force is employed in agriculture, and another 20% is employed in manufacturing and mining. The majority of the country's workers are employed by the service sector. There is much potential for growth, however.

Throughout the 1990s Jordan's economy has regularly outpaced the economies of its neighbors. Consider these GDP numbers:

1992 — Jordan's GDP grew by 16.1%, which was the highest in the region that includes the Middle East and North Africa.

1993 — Jordan's GDP grew by 5.9% against a regional average of 4.8%.

1994 — Jordan's economic growth was 8.1%, again besting the region's average of 2%.

1995 — Jordan's GDP rate was 6.4%, still outdistancing the rates of its regional competitors.

1996 — Jordan's growth rate of 5.2% continued to outperform the average of the region.

The country's infrastructure is sound, and the telecommunications system is modern and reliable, particularly within cities. The nation's financial system is also considered to be modern and is comprised of numerous banks that offer consumers and businesses a wide assortment of services and products.

During the last two decades, Jordan has developed as a major regional business center, building on its prime location as a crossroads for the countries of the Middle East. Government policies have sought to capitalize on this location and create a pro-business climate. Jordan also benefits from its membership in the Arab Common Market, as well as bilateral trade agreements with Saudi Arabia, Syria, Qatar, the UAE, Yemen, Oman, Bahrain, Iraq, Sudan, Egypt, Tunisia, Algeria, and Morocco. The nation also maintains trade ties with India, Indonesia, and the European Union.

The Benefits of Jordan's Tax System

In an effort to expand the economy, create jobs, and promote industry, the government of Jordan offers several incentives, many of which include significant tax advantages. Most incentives are aimed at businesses. Under the Foreign Companies Registration Law, foreign companies can establish a Jordan-based branch for conducting business outside of Jordan. While domestic sales are not permitted under this arrangement, the huge markets of other countries of the Middle East offer enormous potential for sales.

Companies that register under the Foreign Companies Registration Law are eligible for several major tax incentives. The most important include:

- A total exemption from income taxes.

- A total exemption from social security taxes.

- A total exemption from the payment of business registration taxes.

- Total exemptions from customs duties on the furnishings and equipment for the Jordanian branch office.

- Total exemptions from duties on the importation of commercial samples.

The Investment Promotion Law, passed in 1995, provides both domestic and foreign investors with additional incentives and tax exemptions. Under the law, foreign investors enjoy the same rights and protections as Jordanian investors in most sectors of the economy, excepting construction contracting, trade services, and mining. The Investment Promotion Law divides the country into three regions — A, B, and C — based on economic development. Each region enjoys specific incentives and exemptions. The amount of an income tax exemption is determined on the location of the project:

- If the project is in a class A development area, 25%.

- If the project is in a class B development area, 50%.

- If the project is in a class C development area, 7%.

- The above projects are also eligible to receive a tax holiday of 10 years.

In addition, incentives are available to non-Jordanian employees of the Jordan-based regional office. These incentives include:

- An exemption from income tax.

- An exemption from social security tax.

- An exemption on customs duties on household furniture.

- Duty-free importation of a car every two years.

A few final tax facts are noteworthy:

- Jordan's income tax rates are quite competitive —

  — 15% if a company's income is derived from operations in priority sectors such as hotels, mining, manufacturing, and hospitals.

  — 35% for banks, insurance, financial, and similar institutions.

  — 25% for all other companies.

- To be subject to Jordanian income tax, foreign nationals must spend more than 183 days in the country.

- Regarding individual income tax — 50% of a salary paid by the government or a public institution and 25% of a salary paid by the private sector are exempt from personal income tax.

Should you wish to find out more information about the incentives Jordan offers, contact:

The Embassy of Jordan
3504 International Drive, NW
Washington, D.C. 20008
Tel: 202-966-2664
Fax: 202-966-3110

The Jordan Information Bureau
2319 Wyoming Ave., NW
Washington, D.C. 20008
Tel: 202-265-1606
Fax: 202-667-0777

The Ministry of Industry and Trade
P.O. Box 2019
Amman
Jordan
Tel: 962-6-663191
Fax: 962-6-603721

The Free Zones Corporation
P.O. Box 20036
Amman
Jordan
Tel: 962-6-644589
Fax: 962-6-644821

The Ministry of Information
P.O. Box 1845
Amman
Jordan
Tel: 962-6-642311
Fax: 962-6-648895

The Amman Chamber of Commerce
P.O. Box 287
Amman
Jordan
Tel: 962-6-666151
Fax: 962-6-666155

Madeira

Known as the "Pearl of the Atlantic," Madeira is a group of islands that enjoys a prominent position near the east Atlantic's major shipping lanes. It is indeed a "pearl," possessing a delightful climate and a government that has formulated practical policies to promote business. Major tax incentives are provided to companies that conduct their operations in Madeira's International Business Center (MIBC).

The Madeira Islands, which are volcanic, have an area of 286 square miles (741 square kilometers). The island group lies about 625 miles from Lisbon and 545 miles from Africa. The islands form the Portuguese district of Funchal, however, they constitute an autonomous region. It is because of this autonomy that the Madeiran government has been able to enact measures that foster the diversification of the region's economy, as well as encourage international investment.

Madeira's climate is considered to be mild Mediterranean. There are no extremes of temperature or precipitation. Average summer temperatures are about 70 degrees F (22 degrees C) and average temperatures in winter hover around 60 degrees F (16 degrees C). Winter generally receives more rain than summer, but not enough to be considered a rainy season. With its marvelous weather, and remarkable beauty, tourism has become a major component of the region's economy. Several cruise ships stop in Madeira, their passengers enjoying the numerous fine hotels, restaurants, and boutiques that are located on the island.

Although Madeira is officially a part of Portugal, its residents come from many lands. Many current residents, for example, are descended from English, and while Portuguese is the principal language of many of the residents, both Portuguese and English are commonly used in business. Most of the residents, if not fluent in English, speak English as a second language.

The standard of living on Madeira is good, comparable to the quality of life in Portugal and many European countries. The region has a modern infrastructure and quality telecommunications system. Seaports and airports are modern and efficient. Spacious homes and comfortable apartments are available at reasonable prices, and residents enjoy the conveniences that are available in any advanced land.

Madeira: Yesterday and Today

Madeira was known to ancient explorers and traders and is mentioned in Roman records. History, however, credits its discovery to the Portuguese explorer Joao Goncalves Zarco in 1419, who officially claimed the island for Portugal in 1420. A year later, the Portuguese founded the city of Funchal. For the next century and a half, Portugal controlled Madeira, which benefited from its proximity to early shipping lanes and its wonderful climate. When Spain gained dominion over Portugal in the late 1500s, it also assumed control of Madeira. From 1580 until 1640 the Spanish maintained control, losing the island only when Portugal regained its independence. During the Napoleonic Wars, Portugal sided with the British and English troops were sent to help defend the island and protect the shipping lanes of the Atlantic. Many of these British soldiers remained after Napoleon was defeated and married island women. Their descendants helped to establish an important British legacy on the island.

Madeira's traditional economy was based largely on tourism, and products that included flowers, Madeiran wine, tropical fruits, and embroideries. By the late 1970s, island leaders realized that if Madeira was to prosper and improve its standard of living, the island needed to diversify its economy. Legislation promoting investment and creating a pro-business climate was passed, culminating in 1989 with the Madeira International Business Center (MIBC). The MIBC's purpose, which is to encourage and foster the region's business, concentrates on four major sectors:

- An industrial free trade zone, which includes all trade and industrial activities.

- An offshore financial center, which permits banks and financial institutions to establish operations anywhere in Madeira.

- International services, including various operations such as trading, management, trusts, invoicing, and ship operations.

- An international ship register, through which international shippers benefit from competitive advantages that are among the best in the world.

Madeira's position is of major importance to manufacturers and assemblers who wish to expand their trade into Europe, Africa, and the Americas. The region's membership in the European Union (EC) is yet another major advantage, for membership permits its banks and financial institutions easy access to European financial markets.

The Benefits of Madeira's Tax System

Madeira's assortment of tax incentives are aimed primarily at companies and investors. Many of the incentives are significant and can result in major tax savings.

Incentives available to companies that operate in Madeira's free zone include:

- An exemption from taxes on income derived from operations conducted in the free zone until 2011.

- An exemption from municipal property taxes in regard to income derived from operations conducted in the free zone.

- An exemption from transfer, gift, and inheritance taxes, where applicable, on the acquisition of real estate for purposes of establishing operations in the free zone.

- An exemption from local taxes.

- An exemption from capital gains tax on the sales of fixed assets.

- An exemption from having to withhold taxes from the payment of royalties.

- An exemption from having to withhold taxes from interest on loans from foreign banks and on bonds issued by companies. However, note that such funds must be used only for investment in the free zone.

- An exemption from VAT and custom duties on imported goods, which are to be stored and/or transferred in the free zone.

- An exemption from export quotas.

Individual investors also benefit from incentives, including:

- An exemption from withholding and income taxes on dividends, interest on loans of shareholders, and other types of income received by investors in companies that operate from within the free zone.

- An exemption from transfer, gift, and inheritance taxes in respect of all transfers of shares in the capital of companies that conduct their operations from within the free zone.

Incentives are also available to offshore financial service companies:

- An exemption from corporate taxes on all revenues derived from operations conducted by the branch office. These activities must be conducted exclusively with non-residents in Portuguese territory or with other entities that are established within the free zone.

- An exemption from withholding taxes on revenues paid by branches in the funding of other operations.

The beneficiaries must be non-residents in Portuguese territory or entities established within the free zone.

A company's international branch is also eligible for incentives, most notably:

- An exemption from withholding taxes on revenues that are paid by international branches in the funding of other revenues. The beneficiaries must be non-residents in Portuguese territory or entities operating within the free zone.

Incentives are available for service companies whose operations consist of trading, trusts, and similar businesses. These incentives include:

- An exemption from corporate taxes on income derived from business operations until 2011, provided the business is conducted with entities established within the Madeira International Business Center, or with non-residents in Portuguese territory

- An exemption from corporate taxes on the interest of loans, provided the contracted entities are established within the Madeira International Business Center. **Note**, the loans must be used for operations within the MIBC and the lenders must be non-residents in Portuguese territory.

- An exemption for non-resident shareholders in Portuguese territory from corporate and individual taxes regarding dividends and income from interest and other forms of loans and advances of capital until 2011. Note that dividends must arise from the income of entities derived from operations within the MIBC, excluding the proportion of non-exempt income from business operations carried out in Portuguese territory.

The International Shipping Register of Madeira (MAR) provides shipping companies with special incentives, including the following:

- An income tax exemption on profits earned by the company which owns ships under the Portuguese flag and transports in international waters.

- An exemption from taxes on dividends distributed to shareholders.

- No estate duties on the inheritance of shares in a shipping company.

- No capital gains taxes are payable on the sale or transfer of a ship or shares in a shipping company.

- No income tax is payable on the salaries of officers and crews of vessels operating in international waters.

Without question, Madeira offers numerous substantial incentives to companies and investors. Many of these incentives can considerably reduce tax obligations. Combined with Madeira's pleasant climate, the international mix of its people, and its modern, yet relaxing lifestyle, Madeira emerges as an excellent alternative to many advanced, high-tax countries.

Should you like to find out more information about Madeira, contact the following:

The Portuguese Trade Commission
590 Fifth Ave., 3rd Floor
New York, NY 10036-4702
Tel: 212-354-4610
Fax: 212-575-4737

Madeiran International Business Center — SDM
9000 Funchal
Madeira
Portugal
Tel: 351-91-201333
Fax: 351-91-201399

SDM — Madeira Development Company
Rua Imperatriz Dona Amelia
P.O. Box 4164
9052 Funchal
Madeira
Portugal
Tel: 351-91-225466
Fax: 351-91-228950

Chamber of Commerce
Camara de Comercio Industria da Madeira
Av. Arriaga, 41
9000 Funchal
Madeira
Portugal
Tel: 351-91-230137
Fax: 351-91-222005

Malta

A group of islands located between Italy and North Africa, near the center of the Mediterranean Sea, Malta is an independent republic in the Commonwealth of Nations. Malta is the largest island of an island group that has an overall area of about 122 square miles (316 square kilometers). Malta, itself, is about 95 square miles (246) square kilometers).

The residents of Malta enjoy a pleasant climate highlighted by abundant sunshine — about 300 days per year — and little rainfall. Average annual temperatures range from about 89 degrees F (32 degrees C) in summer to 57 degrees F (15 degrees C) in winter. There are few extremes in Malta's typically favorable weather.

About 370,000 people live in Malta. One of the most diverse ethnic populations in the world, the modern population of Malta has descended from people from around the Mediterranean and Europe and has evolved into a unique homogeneous culture. The Maltese language is a testimony to some of the islands' original people. Based on early Semitic, Maltese is built with a Latin alphabet and grammar. While Maltese is spoken today by many residents, English is an official language and the preferred language of business. Italian, French, German, and Arabic are also spoken, but communication is seldom a problem because much of the population is multi-lingual. A majority of the population of Malta is Roman Catholic, however, many other religions are present on the island.

The standard of living on Malta is excellent, comparable to the living standards of the United Kingdom. The island has a friendly, relaxed lifestyle with numerous leisure activities.

The literacy rate is 90% and education through all levels is free. The University of Malta was established in 1592 and is known for the scope and quality of its programs. Comfortable as well as expansive homes may be found throughout the islands, quality restaurants, hotels, and clubs are available, as are numerous recreational activities including sailing, swimming on Malta's renowned beaches, tennis, and golf. Residents and tourists can also enjoy the casino in St. Julians.

Malta: Yesterday and Today

Malta's earliest inhabitation can be traced back to about 4000 B.C. About 1000 B.C. the islands became a Phoenician colony and were used primarily as a place trading ships would stop to replenish water and food on their voyages throughout the Mediterranean. In time, the Greeks, Carthaginians, Romans, Byzantines, Arabs, Normans, Italians, and British dominated the islands. The British, the last foreign power to rule in Malta, controlled the islands as a colony for over 150 years, finally granting the islands independence in 1964. A result of British authority was the legacy of British tradition. Malta's government is modeled after the British Parliament and the islands' laws are based mostly on British common law. Malta remains a member of the Commonwealth.

Over the last several years, Malta's economy has proven to be as vigorous as it is diversified. Major industries include machinery, high-tech products and electronics, textiles, food and beverages. Tourism and international financial services have also grown to be important sectors of the economy. In support of the islands' economy is a modern infrastructure boasting seaports that utilize some of the region's most modern equipment and a telecommunications system that is equal to those of any advanced country. The islands' financial system is similarly modern and efficient, providing the various services businesses and consumers require.

The Benefits of Malta's Tax System

In an on-going policy of promoting investment in Malta and supporting industry on the islands, the Maltese government has enacted legislation that provides a variety of tax incentives. These incentives are aimed at both individuals and companies.

Incentives for individual investors include:

- Income and capital gains derived from sources outside of Malta are taxable only if the recipient is domiciled and a resident of Malta.

- Expatriates are not subject to capital gains tax.

- Foreign residents are taxed only a small percentage on the amount they bring into the country designated for living expenses.

- Malta has no property, real estate, municipal, or taxes.

Incentives for companies include:

- Companies whose business is at least 95% export-oriented are eligible for a tax holiday of 10 years.

- Accelerated allowances for depreciation.

- Investment tax credits.

- Duty-free importation of parts or materials that are used in export products.

- Duty-free shipment on various products shipped to the EC.

- Reduced tariffs on products exported to the United States.

Malta enjoys a delightful climate, offers an interesting culture blended from peoples around the Mediterranean, and offers several significant tax incentives for both individuals and companies.

Should you be interested in finding out more about Malta, contact the following:

The Embassy of Malta
2017 Connecticut Ave., NW
Washington, D.C. 20008
Tel: 202-462-3611
Fax: 202-387-5470

Malta National Tourist Office
Empire State Building
350 Fifth Ave., Suite 4412
New York, NY 10118
Tel: 212-695-9520
Fax: 212-695-8229

Malta National Tourist Office
280 Republic St.
Valletta CMR 02
Malta
Tel: 22-44-44/5,22-50-48/9
Fax: 22-04-01

Malta Development Corporation
House of Catalunya
Marsamxetto Rd.
P.O. Box 571
Valletta
Malta
Tel: 356-221523
Fax: 356-246408

The Commonwealth of the Northern Mariana Islands

Located in the western Pacific Ocean, the Commonwealth of the Northern Mariana Islands fosters an environment conducive to business. In an effort to attract investment to the islands, the government has enacted a variety of impressive incentives, many of which can substantially reduce the tax burden. Combined with superb economic opportunities and the easy access to the markets of Asia provided by the islands, it becomes clear that the Marianas have much to offer.

An archipelago of numerous islands, the main islands of the Marianas are Saipan, Tinian, and Rota. (Guam, also a part of the island group, is not a member of the Commonwealth. See the previous section "Guam" for more information.) The overall area of the Marianas is about 184 square miles (477 square kilometers). Saipan is the largest island of the group with an area of 47 square miles (122 square kilometer), Tinian is next with an area of 39 square miles (101 square kilometers), and Rota is third in area at 32 square miles (83 square kilometers). Saipan is the principal island, containing the government, a busy seaport, and international airport.

Most of the islands are volcanic. Although elevation varies, some places reach over a thousand feet, with Mount Tapotchau on Saipan being 1,554 feet high (about 520 meters).

The climate of the Marianas, oceanic tropical, reminds one of a Pacific paradise. The average annual temperature is about 83 degrees F (about

28 degrees C), with little variation between summer and winter norms. The wettest time of year comes between July and October, while the months between December and June are the driest. Sunshine is abundant.

The population of the islands is about 45,000, about 90% of which lives on Saipan. Another 5% of the Marianas's residents live on Tinian and Rota, with the rest living on other islands in the group. Various Pacific peoples comprise most of the population, along with Americans, Koreans, Filipinos, Japanese, and Chinese representing important minorities. Given the number of ethnic groups, several languages are spoken throughout the islands, but English, Chamorro, and Carolinian are official languages.

The Mariana Islands have a fine standard of living. The school system is modeled after the schools in the United States, health care is good with people having access to modern health centers, and numerous recreational activities abound. Watersports, world-class shopping, dining, and sightseeing in some of the most beautiful island settings of the Pacific are available. The Marianas provide a fascinating mix of Western and Asian customs and architecture that give the islands a distinctive culture.

The Marianas: Yesterday and Today

Historians believe that the Mariana Islands were first inhabited around 5000 B.C. by people of southwest Asia. By the time Ferdinand Magellan arrived in 1521, the islands were populated by Chamorros and Carolinians. After briefly exploring and naming the islands after Mariana, the Queen of Austria who was also regent of Spain, Magellan restocked his ships with water and food and continued on his journey which he hoped would take him around the world. It took the Spanish another 150 years to begin settling the islands, and from that point Spain remained in control for another 230 years. In the treaty that concluded the Spanish-American War, Spain ceded the island of Guam to the United States, formally ending Guam's political ties to the Marianas. Spain sold the rest of the islands to Germany the next year. After World War I, the League of Nations gave the Marianas to Japan, which retained control until the U.S. seized the islands during World War II. After the war the islands became a U.S.-administered U.N. Trust territory. This political structure continued until 1975 when the residents of the Northern Marianas voted to become a commonwealth in association with the U.S. The islands became self-governing in 1978 and residents gained U.S. citizenship in 1986.

Commonwealth status results in a unique political situation for the Northern Marianas. Residents benefit from all the advantages and protections of the U.S. Constitution, as well as many programs of the U.S. government, yet remain self-governing.

Since the late 1980s, as a result of increased U.S. public and private investment, the establishment of direct air service from Japan, which fueled tourism and led to an expansion of tourism-related industries, and the general economic expansion of the economies of the western Pacific, the economy of the Northern Marianas has grown significantly. Even the Asian economic slowdown of the late nineties has not erased the great gains achieved by the Marianas. Aware that continued growth will be built upon economic diversification, the government of the islands has passed legislation that encourages investment.

The infrastructure of the islands is generally good, but the rapid expansion of the economy in recent years has outpaced the government's ability to modernize. Improvements, however, are continually being made. Saipan, Tinian, and Rota each have modern airports and seaports, with the busiest and most extensive located at Saipan. The financial system of the islands is considered to be solid, providing a variety of modern services for both businesses and consumers.

The Benefits of the Marianas's Tax System

Desiring to attract investment to the islands, the government of the Commonwealth of the Northern Mariana Islands has enacted legislation that provides numerous incentives. While most of the incentives are aimed at businesses, individual investors are also able to benefit. The most significant of the incentives include:

- A rebate of up to 95% is possible on taxes paid on both personal and corporate income, provided that such taxes as paid don't surpass $7.5 million.

Note that specific residency requirements must be satisfied to take advantage of this incentive.

- When conducting businesses from a location in the Commonwealth, foreign sales corporations are eligible for federal tax reductions on a part of the income they generate from the sales of exports. Furthermore, they do not have to pay tax to the government of the Commonwealth.

- All ports of entry are free of U.S. Customs duties.

- Specific goods may be exported to the U.S. duty-free and without quota restrictions.

The Commonwealth also offers other major benefits, including:

- A free market system.

- An exemption from U.S. minimum wage laws.

- Visa free borders.

- An exemption from the federal Jones Act, U.S. Merchant Marine Act.

- Intellectual Property Rights are protected under U.S. federal trademark and copyright laws.

If you would like to learn more about the Commonwealth of the Northern Mariana Islands, contact the following:

Office of the Governor
Administration Building
Capitol Hill
Saipan, MP 96950
Tel: 670-322-5091-92
Fax: 670-322-5096

Saipan Chamber of Commerce
P.O. Box 806 CHRB
Saipan, MP 96950
Tel: 670-233-7150
Fax: 670-233-7151

Department of Commerce
Commonwealth of the Northern Mariana Islands
Caller Box 10007 CK
Saipan, MP 96950
Tel: 670-664-3000
Fax: 670-664-3066/67

Mexico

Representing a huge potential market with significant resources just south of the United States, Mexico offers opportunities for both individual investors and companies. Mexico is a large country, almost three times the size of Texas and has an area of 761,604 square miles (1,972,550 square kilometers) that includes coastal lowlands, high plateaus, and towering mountains. In some areas of the north desert-like conditions prevail, while in the southern part of the country, dense rain forests are nurtured by tropical heat and humidity. Perhaps the country's most distinctive geographical feature is the Central Plateau which averages between 5,000 and 8,000 feet (1,500 to 2,400 meters) and is the site of Mexico City, the country's capital.

Extending far more north to south than east to west, Mexico has numerous climates, which vary both because of latitude and altitude. In coastal regions, the weather is generally humid and hot, with the Yucatan Peninsula being tropical. Temperatures on the Central Plateau may average 5 to 15 degrees less than in the Yucatan and even less than that in high elevations. Precipitation also varies, generally being abundant in the far south and decreasing as one travels northward.

Mexico has a population of over 95 million that is increasing rapidly and straining the nation's ability to provide adequate services. The converse of a growing population's demands for services is that Mexico also represents a huge potential market. Of its people, about 60% are Mestizos, 30% are Amerindians, and 9% are descendants of white Europeans. The remainder of the population is comprised of various minority groups. Mexico's official language is Spanish, however, several Mayan tongues are also spoken throughout the country, particularly in remote areas. About 90% of Mexico's people are Roman Catholics, with most of the rest being Protestants. Some Indians in isolated areas still follow Mayan traditional beliefs.

The standard of living in Mexico varies. While residents of many remote areas suffer from poverty and inadequate services, residents of other parts of the country, particularly around the cities, enjoy excellent lifestyles with quality health care, fine educational opportunities, and numerous recreations. Tourist sites, Acapulco for example, offer world-class accommodations, amusements, and entertainment. Mexico, without question, possesses spectacular scenery, beautiful beaches, and a marvelous mixture of history and culture that is distinctive and fascinating.

Mexico: Yesterday and Today

Mexico's history begins with some of the most prominent Indian civilizations of the Americas, including the Toltecs, Mayans, and Aztecs. When the Spanish arrived in Mexico in the early 1500s, they found an impressive Aztec Empire that controlled much of modern Mexico. Although the Aztecs were known for their warlike nature, they proved no match for the Hernando Cortez and his Conquistadors, who conquered Mexico in 1521. The Spanish soon established a colony, which they continued to control until Mexico gained independence and declared itself a republic in 1823.

Mexico's history from that point has been one of slow progress toward democratic rule interrupted by dictatorships, foreign wars, and civil wars. One of the country's greatest burdens has been its unequal distribution of wealth, which many reformers since the early days of colonization have addressed. A turning point came in 1917 after the Mexican Revolution, when a new constitution was adopted and extensive social reforms were initiated. While Mexico has made much progress, the nation's leadership realizes that more steps must be taken. It is attempting to improve the country's quality of life for all citizens through an expansion of the economy.

Mexico clearly has many factors in its favor. Through a change in the government's general outlook regarding business practices, the private sector is growing in importance and influence. Mexico is rich in mineral wealth, including silver, gold, lead, and zinc; the country is equally rich in oil and natural gas. Industry accounts for about 30% of the nation's economy and includes such areas as petroleum refining, iron and steel production, chemicals, mining, textiles and clothing, food and beverages, and the assembly of motor vehicles. The tourism sector is also a major sector of the economy and is expected to continue growing.

Mexico's infrastructure is generally considered to be solid in and around the cities, however, efficiency declines as one moves to outlying regions. The overall telecommunications system is modern and reliable, again, particularly near the cities, less so in isolated areas. The country also has numerous sea- and airports, most of which are equipped to handle modern commerce and travel.

Although the government has taken steps to ensure that the country's banks and financial system are sound, one should regard Mexico's overall financial condition and practices with some skepticism. As recently as 1994, the government was forced to devalue the peso and the United States had to commit funds to ensure that Mexico's currency didn't collapse.

Without question, investors who consider Mexico need to carefully evaluate the pros and cons. Mexico is not as safe for investing as many other places, however, opportunities are available as the government offers some major incentives to encourage investment.

The Benefits of Mexico's Tax System

In the past, many investors dismissed Mexico as offering few worthwhile benefits, particularly in light of the country's potential drawbacks. That has changed in recent years, however, as legislation enacted over the last few years has created numerous powerful incentives that have resulted in Mexico becoming an attractive site for investment. Both individuals and companies are eligible for benefits.

The most important for individuals include:

- Tourists are not considered to be taxable residents in Mexico. Since individuals may reside in Mexico as tourists for up to six months, they are not subject to tax. Many individuals reside in Mexico on a semi-permanent basis, leaving the country for one day every six months.

- Income derived from royalties on copyrights for literary, artistic or scientific works, including film, radio, and TV productions are subject to a tax rate of 15%. This is much less than the standard rate.

The most important benefits for companies include:

- Industries located in free zones may import materials and goods duty-free.

- Assembly plants whose operations are primarily export-oriented may be entitled to duty-free importation of goods for assembly and finishing.

- Certain companies may qualify for immediate investment depreciation. Such companies may, during the first or second year of operation, take an option of a one-time depreciation deduction of their fixed assets. There are some exclusions to this option, including companies located in Mexico City and surrounding areas, Guadalajara, and Monterrey. Also excluded are purchased automobiles, and transportation and office equipment, except computer equipment and peripheral devices. The depreciation rate for industrial bays is 62%, and for machinery and equipment 62% to 95%, depending upon the sector.

- Companies whose operations focus on agriculture, stock breeding, forestry, and fishing are exempt from corporate income tax, provided their profits are reinvested.

It is also noteworthy that the corporate rate for income tax in Mexico is 34%, which is lower than the rate of many other countries, including the United States, Canada, the United Kingdom, Germany, and Japan.

Investors should look upon Mexico with a critical eye. There are, without doubt, drawbacks to investing in Mexico, however, there also are opportunities in the form of tax incentives that can result in considerable savings.

Should you be interested in learning more about Mexico and the opportunities it offers investors, contact the following:

The Mexican Embassy
1911 Pennsylvania, Ave., NW
Washington, D.C. 20006
Tel: 202-728-1600

The Mexican Government Tourist Office
405 Park Ave., Suite 1401
New York, NY 10022
Tel: 212-755-7261 or 800-446-3942
Fax: 212-753-2874

The Mexican Government Tourist Office
181 University Ave., Suite 1112
Toronto M5H 3M7
Canada
Tel: 800-263-9426

The Mexican Consulate
3220 Peachtree Road, NE
Atlanta, GA 30305
Tel: 404-266-1913
Fax: 404-266-2309

The Mexican Consulate
2401 West 6th St.
Los Angeles, CA 90057
Tel: 213-351-6800/07
Fax: 213-389-6864

The Mexican Consulate
27 East 39th St.
New York, NY 10016
Tel: 212-217-6400
Fax: 212-217-6493

The Mexican Consulate
World Trade Center Building
2 Canal Street, Suite 840
New Orleans, LA 70130
Tel: 504-522-3596/97
Fax: 504-525-2332

Monaco

Located in southeastern France, Monaco is a small independent principality and well known resort. Surrounded entirely by France, except on the south where the enclave is bordered by the Mediterranean Sea, Monaco is only 0.7 square miles (1.8 square kilometers) in area. Despite its size, the principality is divided into five sections: Monaco, the capital, La Condamine, the harbor, Monte Carlo, site of the famous casino, Fontvieille, and Moneghetti.

The climate of Monaco features abundant sunshine, mild winters, and warm summers. Average winter temperatures are about 46 degrees F (*8 degrees C*), and average summer temperatures are about 77 degrees (*25 degrees C*).

Of Monaco's resident population of 30,000, about 12,000 are French, 5,000 are Italian, and 5,000 are Monegasques. Other ethnic Europeans make up the rest. Most of the people are Roman Catholics. The official language of the principality is French, however, Monegasque, a hybrid of French and Italian, is spoken by much of the population. English is also widely spoken.

Monaco is known for the overall wealth of its population and standard of living, which is among the best in the world. In many cases, however, living costs are surprisingly reasonable. A pleasant seaside apartment, for example, can be had for as little as U.S.$1,000 per month, which is quite attractive when compared to the excessive costs of apartments in many of the world's major cities. Monaco offers a wonderful lifestyle with numerous recreations, including health clubs, golf, tennis, sailing, and gambling. Being so close to the grand cities of Europe offers the chance for delightful diversions.

Monaco: Yesterday and Today

The first inhabitants of Monaco, for which there is historical evidence, are the Monoikos, a Ligurian tribe from whom the name Monaco likely originated. The Monoikos occupied the site as early as 600 B.C.

After the dominance of the Monoikos passed, no one paid much attention to Monaco until the late 1200s when rival Italian families were locked in a power struggle. In 1297 a Genoese family, the house of Grimaldi, gained control of the fortress that had been built where the present prince's palace stands. The Grimaldis remained in control of Monaco until 1793 when France annexed the enclave. As a condition of the Treaty of Vienna in 1815, Monaco was made a protectorate of the Kingdom of Sardinia until 1861 when it became an independent state under the guardianship of France. In 1911, Prince Albert I granted the enclave a constitution. The constitution has been modified several times, each time reducing the power of the sovereign. Today the power of government is shared by the Prince and a National Council of 18 members.

Monaco has a strong economy. Tourism, banking, insurance, electronic equipment, cosmetics, pharmaceuticals, and gambling are major sectors. Monaco's infrastructure is of high quality, and the principality's financial system is designed to handle the needs of both ordinary and wealthy clients.

The Benefits of Monaco's Tax System

Although Monaco does not offer many tax benefits, it does offer some notable ones, including:

- The principality has no personal income tax, except for French nationals under specific conditions.

- No tax is due for gift or inheritance between husband and wife and between parents and children.

- Neither the Monegasque Fund, nor its investors, are subject to income tax or capital gains tax on the investment. This is based on legislation of 1988.

- Based on legislation enacted in 1991, companies created after October 1, 1991, whose share capital is held less than 50%, either directly or indirectly, by other companies, are exempt from business income tax for the two years of operation and are subject to a reduced tax rate for the next three years.

- Monaco also provides locally tax-free administration of closely-held investment trusts.

If you interested in finding out more about Monaco, contact the following:

Monaco Government Tourist and Convention Bureau
845 Third Ave.
New York, NY 10022
Tel: 212-759-5227
Fax: 212-754-9320

Direction du Tourisme et des Congress de la Principaute de Monaco
2a Boulevard des Moulins
MC 98030 Monaco Cedex
Tel: +377-92-16-61-16
Fax: +377-92-16-60-00

Nicaragua

The largest country of Central America, Nicaragua also may offer the greatest potential and opportunity for investors in the region. With an area of 50,193 square miles (about 130,000 square kilometers), Nicaragua is slightly bigger than the state of New York. Having access to the Caribbean Sea on the east and the Pacific Ocean on the west enables the country to tap global markets. Nicaragua's topography features coastal lowlands that rise to mountains, some of which approach 7,000 feet (about 2,200 meters) and dominate the interior in a north-south direction.

With varying elevations, Nicaragua's climate is rather diverse. Coastal areas are tropical with hot and humid conditions prevailing much of the year, while temperatures and humidity are lower in higher altitudes. The average annual temperature of lands along the coasts is about 78 degrees F (26 degrees C), while in highlands and mountains annual temperatures average 5 to 15 degrees cooler. A rainy season is common from May to October with the greatest amounts of precipitation occurring along the Caribbean coast.

Nicaragua has a population of about 4.3 million, giving the country a generally low population density. Of the population, about 70% are Mestizos, 16% are ethnic Europeans, 9% are of African descent, and 5% are descended from native Indian groups. Spanish is the country's official language, however, English is rather common, especially among the educated in the cities. Indian languages are also spoken, but mostly in outlying regions. The country's overall literacy rate is about 65%. About

90% of the population are Roman Catholics with the remainder being Protestant.

The standard of living in Nicaragua lags behind those of advanced countries, except in major cities, most notably Managua, the capital, and Leon. Although the quality of health care in the cities is good, quality and access decline as one moves to remote areas. For those of the upper classes, Nicaragua is a pleasant place to live. The violence that was once rampant in the country has largely disappeared with only isolated rural areas still experiencing the acts of bandit groups. The nation's cost of living is low compared to Western norms, and there are plenty of recreational activities including fishing, swimming, hiking, surfing, sightseeing, shopping, and dancing. Excellent housing can be obtained in residential areas.

In a program to encourage both domestic and foreign investment, the government of Nicaragua has enacted legislation designed to foster business. This legislation has various incentives, including major tax concessions.

Nicaragua: Yesterday and Today

The Spanish arrived in the land that was to become Nicaragua in 1552 and seized control from the Indian tribes that were settled throughout the region. Spain established a colony which it controlled until 1821 when Nicaragua achieved independence. After being united with Mexico for a short time, and then a part of the United Provinces of Central America, Nicaragua formally became a republic in 1838. In the years that followed the country experienced unrest and turmoil as democratic forces struggled with dictatorships and military takeovers. Periodic unrest continued well into the latter part of the 20th century, culminating in the overthrow of the Somoza regime and subsequent civil war between the Sandinistas and the Contras. Only with the ending of the conflict was the country able to finally make marked strides toward democracy and start to rebuild its economy.

The current government of Nicaragua is based on a constitution adopted in 1987. The country is a republic that guarantees universal suffrage.

Realizing that the country's future depended upon a strong economy, Nicaragua's leadership developed a program of economic stabilization in the early 1990s aimed at decreasing the high rate of inflation (brought down from 750% to less than 5%). Once stabilized, the economy began to improve.

Nicaragua's economy is built around several key sectors, including agriculture, food processing, tourism, chemicals, textiles, metal products, and oil refining. The country grows various crops — bananas, coffee, sugar, cotton, corn, cocoa, rice, tobacco, and fruit are the most important — many of which are exported, and also possesses significant mineral deposits of gold, silver, copper, and tungsten. It is likely that the country has undiscovered deposits of valuable minerals in remote areas.

In recent years the Nicaraguan GDP growth rate has averaged about 4%, with a rate of 5% in 1997, and an expected rate of 6% in 1998. The economic expansion has been stimulated by the export sector, construction, and agriculture. Investment, both private and domestic, is increasing. Despite the growth in GDP, however, the economy is undermined by an infrastructure that needs to be improved. Except for the major cities, the telecommunications system needs to be modernized, roads outside the cities may be in disrepair or unpaved, and sea- and airports lack modern equipment. The government is attempting to improve the country's infrastructure, but improvements are somewhat slow.

Of most importance to investors is the Nicaraguan government's commitment to privatization and opening the country to foreign investment. Since the early 1990s, almost all price controls that had been in place for years have been phased out, more than 300 state enterprises have been privatized, and the government has developed a pro-foreign investment climate. The Foreign Investment Law, for example, allows 100% foreign ownership in all sectors of the economy. Estimates indicate that over the last two years, in-flowing foreign direct investment has doubled from $70 million in 1995 to $133 million in 1997. Close to one-third of the total has come from U.S. companies.

The Benefits of Nicaragua's Tax System

The government of Nicaragua has passed legislation that offers valuable incentives to investors and companies in its effort to attract investment and build the country's economy. The incentives are associated with the country's free trade zones. Along with the state-owned Las Mercedes Industrial Free Zone located near Managua's International Airport, there are two private free zones. Four other free zones have been authorized.

Significant tax incentives are provided for companies that operate from within free trade zones, including:

- A full exemption from income taxes for the first 10 years of operation, and a 60% exemption thereafter.

- An exemption from import duties, levies, and sales taxes on imports.

Another incentive for companies includes a flat tax rate of 30% on Nicaraguan-source income. Beginning in July, 1999, this rate will be reduced to 25%. These rates are lower than the rates of many other countries.

Should you like to learn more about the opportunities in Nicaragua, contact:

The Embassy of Nicaragua
1627 New Hampshire Ave., NW
Washington, D.C. 20009
Tel: 202-939-6570

The U.S. Embassy Managua
Unit 2703 Box 2
APO AA 34021
Tel: 505-266-2291
Fax: 505-266-9056

Nicaraguan American Chamber of Commerce
444 Brickell Ave., Suite 51-168
Miami, FL 33131
Tel: 305-448-2495
Fax: 305-375-0362

Ministry of Economy and Development
Frente Al Centro Comercial Camino de Oriente
Managua
Nicaragua
Tel: 505-267-0002
Fax: 505-267-0041

Ministry of Tourism
Antojitos 1 C. abajo y 1 C. al sur
Managua
Nicaragua
Tel: 505-228-1238
Fax: 505-228-1187

The Free Trade Zones Administration
Km. 12-1/2 Carretera Norte
Managua
Nicaragua
Tel: 505-263-1530
Fax: 505-263-1700

Panama

Positioned between Costa Rica to the north and Colombia to the south, Panama is the southernmost country of North America, connecting that continent to its southern counterpart. Panama is also the site of the Panama Canal that links the Atlantic and Pacific, making the country perhaps one of the most important of the world's crossroads.

Panama has an area of 29,762 square miles (77,082 square kilometers), spread throughout a long narrow country that runs mostly north to south. Sea-level coasts give way to hills and plains, which in turn rise up to mountains that stretch through the nation's interior.

Panama lies fully in the tropical zone and its climate reflects this location, generally being hot and humid, with slightly lower temperatures in the mountains. A rainy season occurs from May to January, while drier conditions are common the rest of the year. The east coast receives about 117 inches (297 centimeters) of rain per year, however the west coast's rainfall averages about half of that amount.

The population of Panama is close to 2.7 million. Of the total, about 70% are Mestizos, 14% are West Indians, 10% are white, and 6% are Indians native to the land. Close to 85% of the residents are Roman Catholics with the rest being Protestants. Spanish is the country's official language, however, English is common and many residents speak both Spanish and English.

Panama's standard of living is generally higher than most countries of Latin America, due, in great part, to the long involvement of the United States with the Canal. Along with building the Canal, Americans also invested heavily in Panama's infrastructure, particularly roads, bridges, hospitals, and schools. That the Canal remains as efficient today as it was in the past is testament to the commitment of the United States, which has resulted in long-term benefits for the Panamanian people. The system of health care is considered good, and the educational system is among the best in the region. Attracted by Panama's location, the industries associated with the Canal, and the nation's solid infrastructure, many businesses over the years have established a presence in the country.

A wide range of recreational activities can be enjoyed in Panama. Swimming, surfing, fishing, sailing, mountain climbing, shopping, fine restaurants and clubs provide pleasure for just about everyone. Of course, many visitors and residents alike find the most pleasure through simple relaxation in Panama's scenic environment. Panama City, the capital, for example, is a busy center of commerce and trade, a wonderful mix of modern energy and architecture graced by colonial gentility.

Panama: Yesterday and Today

The Spanish arrived in Panama early in the colonial period, quickly overcoming the original Indian tribes they encountered, and established a settlement at Nombre de Dios in 1510. As colonization increased, it wasn't long before Panama became vital as a route between Peru, Spain, and Spain's other colonies throughout the New World.

In 1821, Panama broke free of Spain and voluntarily became a part of Colombia, which also had recently gained its freedom. The Panamanians, however, soon became disenchanted with Colombian rule and Panama broke away in 1840. The Colombians, having come to view Panama as a part of their country as well as realizing the importance of the isthmus, regained authority in 1842. The following years were uneasy ones and many Panamanians agitated for independence.

American presence in the region began in 1842 when Colombia signed a treaty with the United States, granting Americans the right to build a railroad across Panama. The railroad became a land bridge from America's east coast to the west.

While the railroad was an advantage to commerce and travel, most planners realized that a far more economical way across the isthmus was a water route. Indeed, the idea of a canal through Panama had been conceived as early as the 16th century, but the engineering and technology needed were well beyond the builders of those days. By the 1880s, however, the French thought the idea was feasible. After obtaining permission from the Colombian government, the French began work in 1880, but they failed, losing 22,000 men to accidents and disease. Interested in a way to link the coasts of the United States by water, American officials offered to continue the project, buying the concession from the French who by this time were eager to sell. Colombia, however, was now embroiled in a civil war and refused to sign a treaty that gave the U.S. the right to assume control of building a canal.

Fortune soon fell to the U.S. When Panama declared itself once again independent of Colombia, the U.S. quickly recognized the new country and signed a treaty with its leaders that gave the U.S. the right to build the canal. After signing the treaty, the U.S. was quite willing to guarantee Panama's independence. The Panamanians, desperate for the U.S. guarantee, granted the U.S. foreign rights in perpetuity over the Canal Zone, as well as the right to intervene in Panama's internal affairs when the U.S. deemed those affairs might threaten the Canal. In the following years, such provisions led to much tension between the two countries, particularly during American interventions, as recently as 1989, for example, when the U.S. military invaded Panama and forced the dictator Manuel Noriega from power. The U.S. has agreed to return all rights of the Canal to Panama, the formal process of which has already begun.

After Noriega, democracy in Panama was restored. Panama today is a republic whose citizens enjoy universal suffrage and a judicial system based on civil laws.

Although the country's economy is built around commerce, tourism, and banking, in recent years a highly sophisticated financial system has developed and the country has been emerging as a major financial center providing international banking services. Of these services, the establishment and management of offshore trusts and corporations are two of the most important to many investors.

The Benefits of Panama's Tax System

Panama has relatively high tax rates on local income, however, the country does offer valuable incentives.

For individuals and corporations:

- No tax on foreign-source income.

Other incentives are designed to attract investment that supports and enhances tourism. Virtually any business that engages in a tourist-related enterprise — hotels, motels, inns, specialty shops, tourist agencies, tourist transportation, restaurants, and clubs are just some examples — may be eligible for the following incentives:

- An exemption from taxes on assets or capital.

- An exemption of up to 20 years on real estate taxes.

- An exemption from income tax on interest earned by creditors in a business operation for investing in hotels.

- An exemption from income tax for a period of 15 years, provided that a business project is located in one of nine geographical zones set aside for tourist development.

- A reduction of 50% of taxable income for individuals and companies who invest in stocks or bonds that are issued by tourist companies.

A special tax incentive is available to companies that operate in the Colon Free Zone. The free zone is located at the Atlantic entrance to Panama and is home to international companies from around the world. Economic activity generated in the zone approaches a billion dollars a year. While the zone is not entirely tax-free, tax rates are extremely low, as noted:

- Corporate tax rates are 30%, however, this rate is discounted by 90% for companies operating in the zone. This results in a tax rate of 3% on profits derived from materials and products that pass through the zone but which are not then sold in Panama.

- The free zone is duty-free.

Panama also offers investors and companies other important advantages, including:

- Panama's currency is the U.S. dollar; there are no exchange controls.

- Panama has over 140 international banks offering sophisticated services to investors.

- Panama's infrastructure is of high quality.

- Panama's financial services sector is among the best in the world, offering investors and companies superior service and products.

- Panama's time is Eastern Standard Time, making business transactions easy for North and South Americans.

- Panama is known as the "Bridge of the Americas" and the "Crossroads of the World," two descriptions that accurately portray the nation's prime location.

If you would like to learn more about the tax opportunities in Panama, contact the following:

The Embassy of Panama
2862 McGill Terrace, NW
Washington, D.C. 20008
Tel: 202-483-1407
Fax: 202-483-8416

Consulate General of Panama
1212 Avenue of the Americas
10th Floor
New York, NY 10036
Tel: 212-840-2450
Fax: 212-840-2469

Consulate General of Panama
555 Brickel Avenue, Suite 729
Miami, Fl 33131
Tel: 305-371-7031
Fax: 305-371-2907

The Embassy of Panama
151 Slater St., Suite 501
Ottawa
Canada K1P 5H3
Tel: 613-567-1283
Fax: 613-567-1679

The Panama Tourist Bureau
P.O. Box 4421, Zone 5
Panama
Tel: +507-226-7000 or +507-226-3544
Fax: +507-226-3483 or +507-226-6856

The Panama Trade Development Institute
1477 South Miami Ave.
Miami, Fl 33130
Tel: 305-374-8823
Fax: 305-374-7822

The U.S. Embassy in Panama
Avenida Balboa and Calle 38
Apartado 6959
Panama City
Panama
Mailing Address: American Embassy Panama, Unit 0945,
  APO AA 34002
Tel: +507-227-1377
Fax: +507-227-1964

Paraguay

Surrounded by Bolivia, Brazil, and Argentina, Paraguay is a landlocked nation in central South America. A relatively large country with an area of 157,048 square miles (406,752 square kilometers), Paraguay is a little smaller than California. It is a land of low flat plains, wooded hills, great forests, and the Parana Plateau that has an average elevation of 1,000 to 2,000 feet (305 to 610 meters).

Paraguay has a subtropical climate, semiarid in the west and progressively wetter as one moves eastward. While some parts of the west average about 32 inches of rainfall (80 centimeters) per year, the east may receive up to 60 inches (152 centimeters). Asuncion, the capital, averages about 44 inches (112 centimeters). Temperatures in the capital are quite pleasant, averaging about 63 degrees F (*17 degrees C*) in July, the southern hemisphere's winter, and 80 degrees F (*26 degrees C*) in January, which is summer.

About 5.5 million people live in Paraguay, giving the country a low population density. Most, about 95%, are Mestizo; the remainder of the people are whites or Amerindians. About 90% of the population is Roman Catholic, with Protestants making up the rest. Spanish is the country's official language, and the literacy rate is about 92%.

The standard of living in Paraguay is uneven, with the quality of life being generally good in the major cities but declining in outlying areas. Adequate health care is not available to all citizens, especially in remote regions. Plenty of recreational activities and tourist facilities are available in and around Asuncion, including excellent restaurants, parks, and theaters. Activities such as hiking, sightseeing, and fishing are enjoyed by many in a relaxed atmosphere and slow pace of life that are hard to find in many parts of the world.

Paraguay: Yesterday and Today

In 1537 the Spanish established the first permanent settlement in Paraguay, easily subjugating the Indian tribes that lived there. However, unlike many of Spain's colonies, over which the crown exercised tight control, Paraguay was never of major importance and consequently enjoyed more freedom. Indeed, for much of the early colonial period, Jesuit missionaries wielded the greatest power in the colony. So strong did Jesuit influence grow in time that Spain ordered the Jesuits out of the colony (along with the rest of Spain's holdings in the New World) in 1767. Spain reasserted its control over the colony, but again, the authority from the crown was negligible. When all of Latin America began rebelling against Spanish rule, Paraguay, too, declared its independence in 1811, which went unchallenged by Spain.

The road to independence might have been easy, but the building of a country was not. For well over the next hundred years, Paraguay suffered through dictators, wars, and conflict between rival political groups.

During this last decade, Paraguay has made significant strides toward democracy. Basic rights have been supported by the government, censorship has been eliminated, and opposition political parties have been legalized. As Paraguay enters the new millennium, its government is a republic with universal suffrage.

Although the country's economy has grown steadily in recent years, Paraguay lags behind many countries of Latin America in economic output and remains dependent upon agriculture. Thus, the economy is susceptible to external factors such as bad weather or poor harvests. Moreover, many farmers are subsistence farmers, and the majority of workers not involved in agriculture are occupied in the service sector. In an effort to strengthen the economy, the government has taken steps to deregulate business activity, eliminate controls on foreign exchange, reduce tariff levels, reform the tax structure, and introduce tax incentives to attract investment. The government has also initiated policies to reduce inflation, eliminate restrictions on capital flows, and privatize many state industries.

Progress has been slow, however, in part due to a somewhat unstable financial system, which lacks strong controls, and an infrastructure that needs to be modernized. Paraguay's telecommunications system is generally unreliable except in the major cities, and even there the system requires modernization. The nation's airports also need to be updated, and only about 5% of the country's roads are paved. In outlying areas, many roadways become unpassable during heavy storms.

Paraguay is a member of several important trade organizations, including: The Southern Cone Common Market (**MERCOSUR**), GATT, and The World Trade Organization. While membership supports trade, the country is not yet fully positioned to take full advantage of its memberships. However, the country's membership in such organizations is an indication of the government's willingness to take steps necessary to realize Paraguay's economic potential.

The Benefits of Paraguay's Tax System

Unlike many of the other countries and jurisdictions in this book, Paraguay does not offer many tax incentives to investors. However, it is noteworthy that foreign-source income is exempt from Paraguayan taxes. This can be an important incentive for individuals who wish to reside in Paraguay but who have substantial foreign earnings.

Should you be interested in learning more about Paraguay, contact:

The Embassy of Paraguay
2400 Massachusetts Ave., NW
Washington, D.C. 20008
Tel: 202-483-6960
Fax: 202-234-4508

The U.S. Embassy in Paraguay
1776 Avenida Mariscal Lopez
Casilla Postal 402
Asuncion
Paraguay
Mailing Address: Unit 4711, APO AA 34036-0001
Tel: 595-21-213-715
Fax: 595-21-213-728

Peru

Peru is fast becoming an economic success story. In the early 1990s the government of Peru embarked upon an ambitious program designed to expand the nation's economy. The program has resulted in impressive gains. Throughout the nineties, Peru's economy has expanded, with 1994 being a highpoint in which the country's GDP of 12.7% was the world's best. Various factors, including strong government incentives, promise that Peru's economic growth will continue.

Bordering the Pacific Ocean, Peru is the third largest country in South America with an area of 496,225 square miles (1,285,215 square kilometers). Peru is a long, narrow land, extending north to south. A coastal plain, lowlands of the Amazon Basin, and the Andes region are the country's principal geographic zones. The coastal plain, which in some places is about 100 miles (160 kilometers) wide, is home to most of the nation's cities and industries, half of its population, and about 65% of its economy. The Amazon Basin, a part of the world's largest tropical rain forest, is largely uninhabited and unexplored. Peru's rugged mountains average about 12,000 feet (3,600 meters), with the highest points above 22,000 feet (6,700 meters). The mountains, which cover about a third of the country, are mineral rich and contain significant deposits of copper, gold, silver, lead, zinc, and phosphate. Peru's copper reserves are thought to be the largest in the hemisphere, if not the world.

The climate of Peru varies, depending upon latitude and elevation. Lowlands in the rain forest are tropical with high heat and humidity, while conditions at mountain peaks, particularly in the southern part of the country, can be quite cold. The Amazon region receives the greatest amount of rainfall, while coastal regions are semiarid, a result of moist trade winds that blow from the east in this part of the world.

Peru has a population of about 24 million. Close to 70% of its people live in urban areas, with about 8 million residing in Lima, the capital city. Indians, many of whom have descended from the Inca, make up about 45% of the population, Mestizos account for another 37%, whites descended from Spanish comprise about 15%, and the remainder of Peru's people are of African descent. The country's official language is Spanish, however, some Indian languages are also spoken but these are mostly found in the Andes. The literacy rate is over 85%. Close to 90% of the population is Roman Catholic; Protestants, Jews, and Muslims are also present.

The standard of living in Peru is good in the major cities, but declines in quality as one moves to outlying regions. Health care is good in the cities but limited elsewhere. Numerous recreational activities are also available in the cities, especially Lima, which compares favorably to most major cities of the world.

Peru: Yesterday and Today

Long before the arrival of the Spanish, the Inca, known as the "people of the sun," dominated the land that was to become Peru. Historical evidence indicates that the Inca arrived around 1100 A.D. and quickly subjugated the people before them. By the beginning of the 16th century, the Inca had built a vast empire. In 1532, drawn by stories of the great wealth of the Inca, Spanish conquistadors, led by Francisco Pizarro, marched into Peru. The end of the Inca followed soon afterward. Pizarro founded a settlement at what was to become modern Lima, and by the 1580s the Spanish had established a colonial presence that was to remain until 1821 when Peru finally gained independence. Conflict with neighbors, domestic turmoil, and a series of dictators hampered the country's progress toward democracy and economic growth.

In 1993, a new constitution was approved by the country's congress. The constitution divides the government into an executive, legislative, and judicial branch, however, because of special powers granted by the constitution, the executive branch is dominant. The president and all members of congress are elected. Compared to the past, the current government has achieved remarkable stability.

Political stability has enabled Peru's leaders to focus their attention on the country's economy. Peru has developed an open and highly competitive market. A major program of privatization was initiated in 1991 with the Private Investment Law, which was aimed at fostering the private sector in the nation's economy. As of November, 1997, Peru's privatization program has resulted in revenues of more than U.S.$7 billion. It has also brought competition and efficiency to many former government-owned industries.

Peru's economy centers around several major sectors: agriculture, forestry, fishing, mining, and manufacturing. In the future, the government hopes to expand and diversify the economy.

In recent years Peru has developed a pro-business environment in which companies are encouraged to invest in the country. Since 1991,

214

over 130 statutes designed to eliminate and reduce administrative controls over the economy have been passed. Furthermore, in 1991, the Foreign Investment Law was enacted, guaranteeing the equal treatment of domestic and foreign investments and ensuring the rights of foreigners.

Peru's infrastructure, which is undergoing continual improvement, is generally solid and capable of supporting a modern society and its economy. The telecommunications system has been largely privatized and is being rapidly modernized, the country has several sea- and airports able to handle modern commerce and traffic, and the country benefits from the Pan-American Highway that runs north to south. The Trans-Andean Highway, linking Lima and Pucallpa, is another major roadway.

Many investors may remember the hyperinflation that afflicted Peru during the 1980s and into the early nineties. Aware that the stress of inflation severely weakened the country's financial system, the government undertook a successful program to reduce inflation, restoring business and consumer confidence and stabilizing the nation's currency. The financial system today is overseered by the nation's Central Bank, which enjoys independence from the executive branch. In addition, the Supervisory Agency of Banking and Insurance (SBS) further regulates the finance industry through its power to inspect records and impose sanctions.

The Benefits of Peru's Tax System

Realizing that a rising standard of living for its people is built upon an expanding economy, the government of Peru has not only taken steps to liberalize its overall economic policy, but has created numerous incentives to attract investment as well. The most advantageous are linked to duty-free zones.

Industrial zones, located at Chimbote, Ilo, Matarani, Paita, and Trujillo, are designed for companies that produce goods and services for export. They offer the following incentives:

- An exemption from taxes.

- Duty-free entry and exit of products to and from third-party countries.

A tourist duty-free zone is located in Ilo. This area is designated as a place where tourist resources may be developed. The following incentives apply:

- An exemption from taxes.

- The zone enjoys duty-free entry and exit of goods to and from third-party countries.

Special commercial treatment zones, which are designed for companies that carry out commercial activities in association with bonded warehouses, are located in Tacna and Tumbes. The following incentives are available:

- An exemption from taxes, now and in the future.

During the 1990s, Peru has made great strides in reducing inflation, achieving political stability, and laying the foundation for a strong economy. The nation has also reached out to the global community as a member of the following international organizations:

- World Trade Organization (WTO)

- International Monetary Fund (IMF)

- United Nations Development Program (UNDP)

- International Finance Corporation (IFC)

- Economic Commission for Latin America and the Caribbean Andean Community

- Inter-American Development Bank (IDB)

- Asia-Pacific Economic Cooperation (APEC)

- Latin American Integration Association (ALADI)

- International Labor Organization (ILO)

- Organization of American States (OAS)

- World Health Organization (WHO)

Should you like to find out more information about Peru, contact:

Embassy of the United States of America, Peru
Av. La Encalada cdra. 17 s/n
Surco
Lima
Peru
Tel: 51-1-434-3000
Fax: 51-1-434-3037

The American Chamber of Commerce of Peru
Av. Ricardo Palma 836 - Miraflores
Lima
Peru
Tel: 51-1-241-0708
Fax: 51-1-241-0709

Republic of the Philippines

An archipelago consisting of more than 7,000 islands, the Republic of the Philippines is positioned between the Philippine Sea and South China Sea, about 750 miles (1,210 kilometers) east of Vietnam. The Philippines is potentially an outstanding site for investment. The government fosters a pro-business climate and encourages investment through a variety of incentives that provide investors with superb benefits.

The Philippine islands cover a large expanse of the Asian Pacific. The country's total area is 115,830 square miles (about 300,000 square kilometers). Of this area, 11 islands — Luzon, Mindanao, Samar, Negros, Palawan, Panay, Mindoro, Leyte, Cebu, Bohol, and Masbate — have areas of more than 1,000 square miles (2,600 square kilometers) and are home to most of the nation's 75 million people. By far most of the archipelago's islands are small and uninhabited. The islands are volcanic, mountainous, and the entire archipelago is prone to earthquakes. Some 20 active volcanoes are found throughout the region.

The Philippine Islands possess a tropical marine climate. Average annual temperatures range between 80 degrees F (*27 degrees C*) to 94 degrees F (*34 degrees C*). Rainfall throughout the islands is somewhat heavy with an average of 80 inches (200 centimeters) per year, much of it coming during the wet season that runs from June to October. Typhoons (the Pacific "hurricane") are a threat during the typical summer typhoon season.

Of the Philippines 75 million people, the dominant ethnic group is the Christian Malays who account for about 91% of the population. Muslim Malays make up another 4%, and Chinese and other minorities comprise the rest. About 83% of the people are Roman Catholics, 9% are Protestant, 5% are Muslim, and the rest are either Buddhist or belong to other religious orders. Official languages are Pilipino, which is based on Tagalog, and English, which is spoken by much of the population and is the language of government and business. The literacy rate of the Philippines is about 95%. Because of American influence over the years, the Philippines has become the third largest English-speaking nation in the world.

The standard of living in the islands is generally good in the cities for professionals, businessmen, and government officials, but relatively poor for people living in outlying areas and who lack education. Numerous forms of entertainment and recreational activities are available throughout the islands. Fishing, swimming, golf, scuba diving to explore some of the world's most spectacular coral reefs, dining at quality restaurants or shopping in big malls or small boutiques, as well as enjoying the exciting nightlife found in Manila, are just some of the things to do in the Philippines. Furthermore, the cost of living is quite reasonable and excellent housing can be obtained for a low cost.

The Philippines: Yesterday and Today

Historians believe that the first inhabitants of the islands of the Philippines arrived from China and the Malayan Archipelago as long ago as 250,000 years. The islands underwent several migrations thereafter, in which people from southeast Asia, Vietnam, Indonesia, and the Malay Peninsula arrived. As early as 300 B.C. a lively trade was carried on by island dwellers with Arabia, India, and China.

Ferdinand Magellan was the first European to reach the Philippines, and in 1542 the Spanish named the islands "Islas Filipinas" in honor of King Philip, II. Twenty-two years later the Spanish established a permanent settlement and the Philippine Islands became a Spanish colony. At one time or another, several nations, including the English, Dutch, and Portuguese, tried to wrest control of the islands from Spain, but Spain retained its authority, finally ceding the islands to the United States at the conclusion of the Spanish-American War in 1898. Except for a period during World War II when the Japanese seized the islands, the islands remained under the control of the U.S. until 1946 when they gained their independence.

The government of the Republic of the Philippines is modeled closely after the federal government of the U.S. Its laws are based on Spanish and Anglo-American laws.

Built around agriculture and light industry, such as textiles, chemicals, electronics assembly, petroleum refining, pharmaceuticals, and wood products, the economy of the Philippines is able to take advantage of the markets that rim the Pacific. A series of steps taken by the government, begun in 1992, to stimulate investment and strengthen the nation's financial system have had excellent results. In 1994, for example, the gross national product (GNP) expanded by 5.1% and overall growth — despite the Asian recession of 1998 — has been steady since then. Reforms have also been made to liberalize import regulations, restructure tariff requirements, ease foreign exchange, encourage foreign investment, and support privatization. In addition, efforts continue to attract foreign investment, reduce government bureaucracy, and revamp the tax system.

On the whole, the infrastructure of the Philippines is adequate, particularly in and around the cities. Several sea- and airports are capable of handling modern transportation and the telecommunications system is generally considered to be good.

The Benefits of the Philippines's Tax System

Seeking ways to support the country's industrial base, the government of the Philippines has enacted numerous important incentives. Most are designed to encourage companies to invest in the islands.

The Omnibus Investment Code provides incentives to both domestic and foreign investors in high-priority economic activities. The most important of these incentives include:

- An income tax holiday.

- An exemption from national or local contractors' tax.

- The importation of capital equipment and spare parts tax and duty-free.

- A deduction of labor expenses from taxable income.

- A tax credit on capital equipment obtained from local sources.

Companies that establish facilities in areas classified by the government as "less-developed" are eligible for the following incentives:

- A full deduction from taxable income of the costs necessary for infrastructure and public facilities in the area.

- A double-deduction of labor expenses.

Companies that establish facilities in export processing zones are eligible for the following incentives:

- Exemption from local taxes, licenses, and fees.

- An exemption from real estate taxes in regard to production equipment not attached to the land.

- A special tax on merchandise within the zone.

- An exemption from the 15% branch profits remittance tax.

If you would like to find out more about the tax incentives available in the Philippines, contact the following:

The Embassy of the Philippines
1600 Massachusetts Ave., NW
Washington, D.C. 20036
Tel: 202-467-9300
Fax: 202-328-7614

U.S. Embassy in the Philippines
1201 Roxas Boulevard
Ermita, Manila
Philippines
Mailing Address: APO AP 96440
Tel: 632-521-7116
Fax: 632-522-4361

The Philippine Department of Tourism
556 Fifth Ave.
New York, NY 10036
Tel: 212-575-7915

The U.S. Agency for International Development (USAID)
Ramon Magsaysay Center
1680 Roxas Blvd.
Manila
Philippines
Tel: 632-522-4411
Fax: 632-521-5241

The American Chamber of Commerce of the Philippines, Inc. (AMCHAM)
2nd Floor, Corinthian Plaza
Paseo de Roxas
Makati City
Philippines
Tel: 632-818-7911 to 15
Fax: 632-816-6359

Portugal

During the last several years, Portugal's economy has been one of Europe's leaders. For example, between 1986 and 1992, Portugal's average GDP growth rate was 4.6%, among the highest of all industrialized countries. That same period saw direct foreign investment increase from $164 million to $4.4 billion. The country is a potentially excellent site for investment. Since 1986 when Portugal entered the European Union (EU), the country's government has undertaken steps to promote business and open Portugal to world trade. Unquestionably, Portugal today ranks as one of the top investment environments of Europe. The nation has developed a positive business climate, encourages investment, and offers a variety of tax and financial incentives.

Located in the western part of the Iberian Peninsula, Portugal faces the Atlantic Ocean and occupies a prime position that includes trade routes between northern and southern Europe, Africa, the Americas, and Asia. Portugal's area, which includes the islands of Madeira and the Azores, is 35,553 square miles (92,082 square kilometers) and is about the size of the state of Indiana. There is much variety to the country's topography, from an expansive coastal plain to mountains in the interior, of which the range of the Serra da Estrela rises to over 6,550 feet (about 2,000 meters).

The climate of Portugal varies according to latitude and elevation, but on the whole is rather pleasant. While the northern parts of the country, particularly in the mountains have a temperate climate, the lowlands of the south have weather typical of Mediterranean lands. Annual average temperatures range from a high of about 68 degrees F (*20 degrees C*) in the south to about 50 degrees F (*10 degrees C*) in the upper elevations of the north. Rainfall is generally low, with the north receiving more rain than the south, and winters tend to be short and mild. There are few extremes to the nation's weather.

About 10 million people live in Portugal. Most can trace their lineage to Iberians and Moors, and many residents have ancestors from both groups. Close to two million people live in Lisbon, the nation's capital and leading seaport. Portuguese is the national language, however, English is spoken by many of the residents, especially by city dwellers. French is also spoken in many parts of the country but more so in the north. Close to 95% of the population is Roman Catholic, with the rest belonging to Protestant churches.

Portugal's standard of living compares favorably with many of the countries of Europe. Health care is accessible to the population, and education is valued. The University of Lisbon and the University of Coimbra, for example, were both founded in 1290 and have a strong tradition of scholarship and advanced programs.

Portugal offers a lifestyle that has just about everything. The country offers the pleasures of the modern world as well as the charm of the old. Lisbon, for example, is not only a city of business, but of fine restaurants, hotels, museums, shops, and parks. For recreation, you may enjoy swimming, water-skiing, sailing, windsurfing, scuba diving, golf, tennis, fishing, hunting, horseback riding, equestrian shows, and, of course, bullfights. The Algarve, on the country's southern coast, is one of Europe's favorite vacation sites. Portugal clearly has much to offer everyone.

Portugal: Yesterday and Today

Portugal is a land rich in history and tradition. Although various tribes lived in Portugal during Neolithic times, the country's recorded history begins in the 2nd century B.C. when Portugal became a part of the Roman Empire. The country remained under Roman control for much of the next 600 years. In the 5th century A.D., the Germanic tribe of the Visogoths, who later took part in the sacking of Rome itself, spread throughout Portugal. Visogothic feudal lords retained control of much of the country until the 8th century when the Moors, invading from North Africa, seized vast regions of Portugal. Over the next several hundred years, Moors and the original inhabitants remained locked in a struggle for control. Not until 1279 were the Moors finally expelled from Portugal, though they left behind a rich legacy.

After the expulsion of the Moors, Portuguese kings united and strengthened the country and by the 1450s Portugal had become one of the leading powers of Europe. During the 16th century, the country controlled colonies around the world and had far-reaching trade interests. Eventual conflict with Spain severely reduced Portugal's position during the 1600s, and Portugal was never able to recover its world status. From the conclusion of the Napoleonic Wars through World War II, various Portuguese leaders and governments attempted to bring about democratic reforms, however, it was only after civilian rule was finally and firmly established in 1976 that a stable democracy emerged.

Today, Portugal is known as a country that welcomes business and investment. Its economy is recognized as one of the fastest expanding of Europe, as well as one that offers a broad range of opportunities. During the nineties, Portugal's economy has grown and diversified, the amount of foreign investment has increased significantly, and the bureaucracy that once stifled business has been reformed and streamlined. Several sectors contribute to Portugal's GDP: agriculture, 10%, industry, 30%, and services, 60%.

The government's strong promotion of industry in recent years has resulted in numerous companies manufacturing various products, including: automobiles, chemicals, plastics, paper products, rubber, clothing, footwear, textiles, foodstuffs, and beverages, particularly wine. Most manufacturing companies are small or of medium-size, permitting them to respond quickly to their customer's needs.

Since 1986 Portugal has been a full member of the European Union (EU), and since May, 1998, the country has been a member of the European Monetary Union (EMU). Being a full partner in the EU, the world's largest economic market, ensures that there are no restrictions on the free flow of goods, services, or capital between Portugal and other members of the union.

Portugal's economic growth has been the envy of many European countries. From 1985 to 1989, GDP rose an average of 4.4%, more than any other European country. Although growth was slower during the early nineties because of the general effects of Europe's recession, by 1997 Portugal's economy grew at a rate of 3.4%, which was among the fastest expanding economies of the EU. It is noteworthy that the inflation rate was only 1.9%.

The country's infrastructure, although good, is being modernized with major improvements aimed at telecommunications systems and transportation facilities. Some $20 billion has been designated for infrastructure improvement in recent years.

The Benefits of Portugal's Tax System

To encourage investment and promote the nation's economy, the Portuguese government has enacted legislation providing various tax incentives. The most important include:

- Real estate holding companies incorporated during or after 1989 may be eligible for a reduced corporate tax rate of 25% for a period that varies between seven and ten years.

- Only 50% of dividends on shares obtained during a process of privatization are subject to tax for five years after the date of acquisition.

- Large investment projects that are aimed at increasing exports may be eligible for tax incentives on an individual basis.

Along with specific tax incentives, Portugal offers various other incentives. These incentives are usually available for companies that conduct their business in specific sectors.

For certain companies in the manufacturing and mining sectors, the following incentives may be available:

- Cash grants for 30% to 70% of the cost of investment for modernization, the implementation of new technologies, the conducting of research and development, the training of staff in new methods or processes, or the conducting of strategic or feasibility studies.

- Reduced rates of between 40% and 80% for loans aimed at the cost of machinery, construction, and capital associated with start-up operations.

- Cash grants to investment projects initiated by companies that employ fewer than 250 people.

Companies that invest in areas of Portugal that are designated as being underdeveloped are eligible for the following incentives:

- Companies that invest in manufacturing, mining, tourism, or trade may be granted cash and loans at reduced rates. The incentives are made available through the Regional Incentive System (SIR).

Companies that invest with the purpose of modernizing regions of Portugal that are severely affected by changes in the textile and clothing industries are eligible for various incentives, including:

- Support of 40% to 60% of the total costs of investment aimed at increasing the productivity of established companies.

- Support of 40% to 60% of the total costs of investment designed to increase the global competitiveness of Portuguese companies.

- Reduced rates for loans for Portuguese companies that wish to establish operations in other countries.

While the incentives noted above are made available to eligible companies in Portugal, remember that the Azores and Madeira, which belong to Portugal, offer incentives of their own. For more information, refer to the sections about these islands.

If you would like to find out more information about Portugal, contact:

Embassy of Portugal
2125 Kalorama Rd., NW
Washington, D.C. 20008
Tel: 202-328-8610
Fax: 202-462-3726

Consulate General of Portugal
630 Fifth Ave., Suite 310-378
New York, NY 10111
Tel: 212-246-4580
Fax: 212-459-0190

Portuguese Trade Commission
590 Fifth Ave., 3rd Floor
New York, NY 10036-4702
Tel: 212-345-4610
Fax: 212-575-4737

Portuguese National Tourist Office
590 Fifth Ave., 4th Floor
New York, NY 10036-4704
Tel: 212-354-4403
Fax: 212-764-6137

Portuguese Trade and Tourism Office
1900 L St., NW, Suite 310
Washington, D.C. 20036
Tel: 202-331-8222
Fax: 202-331-8236

Portuguese Trade and Tourism Office
88 Kearny St., Suite 1770
San Francisco, CA 94108
Tel: 415-391-7080
Fax: 415-391-7147

Consulate General of Portugal
3298 Washington St.
San Francisco, CA 94115
Tel: 415-921-1443
Fax: 415-346-1440

ICEP — The Portuguese Foreign Trade Institute
Avenida 5 de Outubro 101
1016 Lisboa Codex
Portugal
Tel: 351-1-793-0103
Fax: 351-1-793-5082

Puerto Rico

Puerto Rico, the easternmost island of the Greater Antilles, is located in the Caribbean Sea about 950 miles (about 1600 kilometers) southeast of Miami. Officially known as the Commonwealth of Puerto Rico, several islands comprise the group: the island of Puerto Rico and many smaller islands, the largest of which include Vieques, Culebra, and Mona. The name "Puerto Rico" comes from the Spanish term "rich port," which aptly described the island's 16th century capital and port, San Juan Bautista de Puerto Rico. In time the port came to be known simply as San Juan and the island as Puerto Rico.

Puerto Rico boasts one of the Caribbean's strongest and most diverse overall economies. The island has the third highest per capita income in the Western Hemisphere, trailing only those of the United States and Canada. Furthermore, of all Latin American countries, only Mexico and Brazil have a greater volume in total external trade. The country's economy is largely the result of the government having taken positive steps to promote the island's economy by offering a variety of tax and business incentives.

Roughly rectangular in shape, Puerto Rico has an area of 3,500 square miles (9,100 square kilometers) and is about the size of Connecticut. Much of the island may be described as having coastal lowlands that gradually rise into hills and a mountainous interior, with a central mountain range reaching an elevation of 4,389 feet (1,338 meters).

Despite its relatively small size, Puerto Rico lies within the path of the trade winds and, because of its mountains, possesses several micro climate zones from tropical to semi-arid. Because the trade winds blow from the east, the eastern side of the island and the eastern slopes of the central mountains receive the most rain, while the western slopes and western coast become progressively drier. The abundant rainfall over much of the island accounts for its lush tropical rainforests, and yet, the southwestern coast has a distinct dry season. There is little variation in temperature throughout the year. San Juan, the capital city, averages about 79 degrees F (26 degrees C) annually and is indicative of the temperatures over much of the island. Higher elevations experience lower temperatures, but even these are not extreme.

About 3.8 million people live in Puerto Rico, with close to 1.5 million living in the capital of San Juan. The population is made up of descendants of Native Indians, Europeans, and Africans, resulting in a society whose unique merging of traditions has created an island with an interesting and distinctive culture. Although Spanish and English are official languages, Spanish is the dominant language as well as the language of the government. The importance of English is well recognized, however, and English is taught in the schools throughout all the grades. The literacy rate is about 90%. Most Puerto Ricans, about 80%, are Roman Catholics with many of the rest describing themselves as Protestant.

Puerto Rico provides its people with a fine standard of living. A large, dynamic middle class is the backbone of the society in which the average annual family income is about $25,000 and per capita income is about $7,000. The island offers excellent housing, from seaside apartments to spacious villas, countless fine restaurants and hotels, and nightclubs that feature top bands and dancing. Other activities include swimming, boating, fishing, surfing, skin diving, tennis, golf, and horse racing. Museums, shopping malls, art galleries, and historical sites, along with breathtaking natural beauty, make boredom a rare event on Puerto Rico.

Puerto Rico: Yesterday and Today

The first European to visit Puerto Rico was Columbus in 1493. The Spanish Conquistadors were not far behind. In 1508, Juan Ponce de Leon — who later searched Florida for the fabled Fountain of Youth — established the first permanent Spanish settlement. The Spanish soon dominated the island with their language, culture, religion, architecture, and, of course, military and political systems. That domination lasted for 400 years, until Spain ceded the island to the United States upon conclusion of the Spanish-American War.

American involvement since the early 20th century has greatly benefited Puerto Rico. In 1917 Puerto Ricans were granted U.S. citizenship, permitting easy travel between the island and the U.S. Mainland. The U.S. has also helped to maintain the island's infrastructure, which is one of the best in the region, and countless U.S. companies have invested in the island, taking advantage of its location in the Caribbean. In 1950, Puerto Rico drafted a constitution, based on the U.S. Constitution, modeling its government on that of the U.S. federal system.

Puerto Rico is clearly one of the economic successes of the Caribbean. With a per capita income that is the third highest in the Americas, its people enjoy a better standard of living than the rest of Latin America. The island's strong economic position today can be traced to the late 1940s when island leaders realized that the island's economy had to be expanded and diversified. One of the first steps to this end was the establishment of the Economic Development Administration (EDA) in 1950. The objective of this agency was to assist local and Mainland investors in the establishment of manufacturing operations on the island. To encourage investment, numerous powerful incentives — including tax benefits — were offered. In the years that followed, specific industries were targeted as vital for growth and inducements were refined. The success of this strategy is clear. Note these facts:

- In 1950, only 82 factories were in operation in Puerto Rico; by 1994, over 1,800 were in operation.

- In 1994, manufacturing generated $16.3 billion dollars, about 40%, of the island's GDP.

- Most factories in Puerto Rico are four to six times more profitable than their counterparts on the U.S. Mainland.

- In 1996, Puerto Rico's GDP was more than $45.5 billion.

- Since 1993, the annual growth of the GDP has been 7%.

The economy of Puerto Rico is founded on more than the industrial sector, however. The service sector accounts for close to 40% of the GDP with tourism playing a major role. Close to four million visitors a year come to Puerto Rico, spending more than $1.5 billion. Indeed, the island is one of the prime tourist sites of the Caribbean, with most tourists staying in and around San Juan.

Puerto Rico's infrastructure is generally equal to that of the U.S. Mainland. Its $4 billion telecommunications system is of the highest quality, while its sea- and airports are fully modernized. In part due to its solid infrastructure, the island is emerging as a communications, transportation, and shipping center of the Caribbean.

With major banks from the U.S. Mainland, Canada, and Spain, as well as numerous local financial institutions and investment houses, Puerto Rico is also becoming a regional financial center. It is estimated that the island's financial system controls assets of close to $40 billion. The unit of currency is the U.S. dollar.

The Benefits of Puerto Rico's Tax System

Puerto Rico's tax code provides many superior incentives for businesses, including exemptions, local inducements, trade zones, and wage support. Although most of the incentives are aimed at businesses, obviously, investors in those businesses stand to benefit as well.

Some of the most significant incentives are federal tax exemptions, including:

- Resident individuals and corporations in Puerto Rico are not subject to U.S. Internal Revenue laws, as noted in Section 9 of the Federal Relations Act.

- Corporate profits earned in Puerto Rico receive federal tax credits after profits are remitted to U.S. parent companies, as noted in Section 936 of the U.S. Internal Revenue Code.

Various local tax exemptions are also possible, including:

- Service industries and manufacturers are eligible for an exemption of 90% from Puerto Rico taxes, including state taxes on corporate earnings, real estate, and personal property. These exemptions may remain in effect for a period of 10 to 25 years, depending upon the location of the company.

- Companies may be eligible for an exemption of 60% on excise and other taxes required for licenses throughout the time of the tax exemption.

- Companies may defer their tax-exempt years on an annual basis.

Companies that are engaged in special projects in tourism may be eligible for several special incentives as a result of the Tourism Development Law of 1993. The most significant incentives include:

- Projects may receive an exemption from various taxes for a 10-year period. The exemptions may be renewal for another period of up to 10 years.

- Also, income and dividends from tourism projects are exempted from taxes at a rate of up to 90%. In the islands of Vieques and Culebra, the exemption may be 100%.

- Projects may be eligible for a 50% tax credit in regard to investments.

Two Foreign Trade Zones (FTZ) have been established in Puerto Rico. The FTZ at Mayaguez concentrates on manufacturing, and the one in San Juan is general in its purpose. Both offer considerable incentives and benefits. Located outside U.S. Customs, but within Puerto Rico, companies that operate within the FTZ enjoy the benefits of U.S. jurisdiction as well as the advantages of Puerto Rico's superior infrastructure and location as an exporter to countries throughout the Americas and Caribbean. The following benefits are available to companies in the FTZ:

- An export manufacturing exemption.

- A tax-free and duty-free base within the jurisdiction of the U.S.

It should be noted that all tax-exempt agreements are made between the Puerto Rican government and a company, and such agreements are protected by both Puerto Rican and U.S. laws, ensuring the security of the agreements. Thus, companies need not fear that exemptions may be unexpectedly canceled.

In addition to the various tax incentives already noted, Puerto Rico offers a host of other inducements, most notably local inducements that include cash grants for training purposes, equipment costs, and rent. The Economic Development Administration (EDA) also provides assistance to companies establishing operations on the island.

If you would like to learn more about Puerto Rico, contact the following:

The Puerto Rico Economic Development Administration
1290 Avenue of the Americas
New York, NY 10104
Tel: 212-245-1200

The Puerto Rico Economic Development Administration
1331 Pennsylvania Ave., NW
Washington, D.C. 20004
Tel: 202-662-8977

The Puerto Rico Economic Development Administration
2635 Century Parkway
Atlanta, GA 30345
Tel: 404-321-5284

The Puerto Rico Economic Development Administration
233 N. Michigan Ave.
Chicago, IL 60601
Tel: 312-565-0910

The Puerto Rico Economic Development Administration
10100 Santa Monica Blvd.
Los Angeles, CA 90067
Tel: 213-553-6369

The Puerto Rico Economic Development Administration
355 F.D. Roosevelt Ave.
Hato Rey
Puerto Rico 00918
Tel: 809-758-4747

St. Kitts and Nevis

About a third of the way from Puerto Rico to Trinidad and Tobago lies the two-island nation of St. Kitts and Nevis. Together, their total area is only about 102 square miles (270 square kilometers), but it is not their size that is attractive to investors. Along with their tropical splendor, the small country's tax laws provide the opportunity to reduce one's overall tax burden while at the same time amassing wealth. Furthermore, because of the unique political structure of the islands — Nevis has the right to pass its own laws and retains the constitutional right to secede from St. Kitts — Nevis has evolved into one of the best sites for asset protection trusts.

The climate of the islands is subtropical with little variation in seasonal temperatures, which average about 80 degrees F (*27 degrees C*). Unlike the temperature, however, rainfall does vary. A rainy season occurs between May and November, and a dry season lasts from January to April. Overall rainfall is plentiful at about 50 to 80 inches (125-200 centimeters) per year.

About 41,000 people live on the islands, most of whom have descended from Africans. English is the predominant language and the literacy rate is 97%. Most residents are Christian, belonging either to the Catholic Church or one of several Protestant churches.

The standard of living on St. Kitts and Nevis is good, particularly in the cities and tourist sites. A host of recreational activities are available, including: watersports, boating, sailing, tennis, bicycling, horseback riding, and mountain climbing. Dining and dancing are offered by numerous fine restaurants and clubs, and several duty-free shops offering countless items make shopping a major attraction. Although the islands offer as much in the way of entertainment as other Caribbean islands, they have one thing that many other islands lack — a truly relaxed lifestyle that these days is so hard to find.

St. Kitts and Nevis: Yesterday and Today

In 1493, Columbus came upon St. Kitts and promptly named it after his patron saint, St. Christopher. Columbus then sailed southward, discovering Nevis, which he named Nuestra Senora de las Nieves, "Our Lady of the Snows," because clouds that obscured the island's features reminded him of the Pyrenees Mountains of Europe. Today, the island is simply referred to as Nevis.

The Spanish claimed the islands but never settled them, and in 1623 English settlers established the first successful English base in the West Indies. The French seized the islands several times during the next 200 years, but returned them to England as a stipulation of the Treaty of Paris, 1783. Britain retained control until 1967 when St. Kitts and Nevis became members of the West Indies Associated States. In 1983, the islands formed a federation with their capital at Basseterre, but they retain close ties to Britain. The queen of England is the chief of state, who is represented by the governor general. The governor general appoints the prime minister, who is the actual head of the government. The islands' legislature, the House of Assembly, is elected through universal suffrage. Laws are based on English common law.

The economy of the islands is built around agriculture, tourism, light manufacturing, and, increasingly, financial services. The islands possess a good infrastructure and a modern financial system.

In April of 1997, St. Kitts and Nevis opened the first and only International Financial Center in the Caribbean. This center nicely complements the offshore banking services that are available in Nevis. However, it is in the area of trusts that Nevis has gained the attention of investors.

Since 1994, when the Island Assembly on Nevis adopted the Nevis International Trust Ordinance, one of the most comprehensive and flexible asset protection trust (APT) laws in the world, Nevis has enjoyed well-founded popularity among international investors. Comparable to the superb APT laws of the Cook Islands in the South Pacific, but in many ways more flexible, the primary objective of the law is to allow foreign investors to secure protection against threats to their property and assets through the transfer of title to an APT established in Charlestown, Nevis. A Nevis trust provides a great deal of asset protection, for it places personal assets out of the reach of foreign governments and their agencies, litigious plaintiffs, creditors, and, of course, lawyers.

In accordance with the law, Nevis judges will not recognize any non-domestic court orders regarding APTs established in Nevis. Thus, foreign agencies or creditors must try their suits through the court system of Nevis, regardless of any previous judgments. Moreover, any plaintiff, before suing in Nevisian courts, must post a bond of U.S.$25,000 with the government to cover court and other costs. On top of that, the statute of limitations for filing a legal challenge to a Nevisian APT runs out one year from the date of the creation of the trust. Finally, the law places the burden of proof on the foreign claimant, particularly in cases where fraudulent intent on the part of the trust, its officers, or beneficiaries is alleged.

Confidentiality is also an important feature of an APT on Nevis. Because basic trust documents need not be filed with the Nevis government, and therefore do not appear on the public record, privacy is maintained. The only public information required to establish an APT on Nevis is a standard form or letter that identifies the trustee, the date the trust is established, the date of filing, and the name of the local trust company that represents the APT. A governmental fee of U.S.$200 is required upon filing, with an additional annual fee of U.S.$200 required to maintain the trust.

Yet another advantage of the APT is that, in accordance with the Nevis International Trust Ordinance, the same individual can serve as the creator, beneficiary, and protector of the trust. Being able to act in this triple capacity — which is much more than the trust law in most places permits — allows the individual great control over his or her assets. Nevis law requires appointment of a trust "protector" whose responsibility is to oversee the operation of the trust and ensure that the objectives of the trust are met and that the law is adhered to. However, Nevis law permits the beneficiary to serve as a trust protector as well.

The Benefits of St. Kitts and Nevis's Tax System

St. Kitts and Nevis offer a wide assortment of tax incentives for investors. Some are designed for individuals, while others are aimed at encouraging businesses to establish operations on the islands. The most important incentives include:

- There are no personal income taxes in St. Kitts and Nevis.

- There are no gift taxes, sales tax, or estate duties in St. Kitts and Nevis.

- Corporate tax holidays from 10 to 15 years, depending on the amount of value added in St. Kitts and Nevis, are available for eligible companies.

- A corporate tax holiday for "enclave" industries, companies that produce goods exclusively for export outside the CARICOM region, are available for eligible companies for up to 15 years.

  - Note that upon the end of a tax holiday period, St.Kitts and Nevis provides a further tax concession in the form of a rebate of a portion of the income tax paid, based on export profits as a percentage of total profits. This may range from 25% to 50%.

- For eligible companies, an exemption from import duties on parts, raw materials, and production materials is available.

- Hotel proprietors may benefit from the Hotel Aids Ordinance, which stipulates that the gains or profits of a hotel of more than 30 bedrooms is exempt from income tax for a period of 10 years. Hotels of less than 30 bedrooms may qualify for an exemption of gains or profits for five years.

In addition, the following incentives are available:

- For companies that are registered with the Federation of St. Kitts and Nevis, full repatriation of all profits, dividends, and imported capital is guaranteed.

- As a member of the Caribbean Common Market (CARICOM) St. Kitts and Nevis enjoys duty-free access to other CARICOM countries.

- Through the Lome Convention, St. Kitts and Nevis enjoys privileged access to the countries of the European Economic Union (EEU).

- As a member of CARIBCAN, a Canadian economic and trade development assistance program, St. Kitts and Nevis enjoys duty-free access of most products to Canada's markets.

Should you be interested in finding out more about St. Kitts and Nevis, contact the following:

The Embassy of St. Kitts and Nevis
3216 New Mexico Ave., NW
Washington, D.C. 20016
Tel: 202-686-2636
Fax: 202-686-5740

Government Headquarters — St. Kitts and Nevis
Church St.
Bassetere, St. Kitts
St. Kitts and Nevis
Tel: +1-869-465-2521
Fax: +1-869-465-5202

Financial Services Department — Government of St. Kitts and Nevis
P.O. Box 186 Basseterre, St. Kitts
St. Kitts and Nevis
Tel: +1-869-466-5048
Fax: +1-869-466-5317

St. Kitts Tourist Board
Pelican Mall
Basseterre, St. Kitts
St. Kitts and Nevis
Tel: +1-869-465-2620
Fax: +1-869-465-8794

Nevis Tourist Board
Main St.
Charlestown, Nevis
St. Kitts and Nevis
Tel: +1-869-469-1042
Fax: +1-869-469-1066

St. Martin (St. Maarten)

One of the Leeward Islands in the West Indies, St. Martin is shared by two jurisdictions: Saint-Martin, the northern part of the island, which is a dependency of France, and Sint Maarten, the southern part, which belongs to the Netherlands Antilles and is internally self-governing.

The island has an area of 33 square miles (86 square kilometers) and is the smallest island in the world to be shared by two nations. The area of the French part of the island is about 20 square miles (52 square kilometers) with the remainder belonging to the Dutch. The border between the two parts of the island is open and people may travel freely between both sections. Indeed, this spirit of cooperation has been present for close to 350 years.

St. Martin's climate is tropical but moderated by the northeast trade winds. With abundant sunshine and pleasant temperatures throughout the year, the island has developed into a popular tourist destination. Summertime temperatures average about 82 degrees F (*28 degrees C*) and dip only a few degrees during the winter months. About 45 inches of rainfall (110 centimeters) is the annual average with the greatest precipitation occurring during the late summer and early fall.

A total of some 50,000 people live on the island, with about 32,000 Dutch residents and 28,000 French. The ethnic makeup of the population is varied with people tracing their ancestry to Africans, English, Spanish, Portuguese, and of course Dutch and French. Roman Catholicism, various Protestant sects, and Judaism (though somewhat of a minority) comprise the major religions. Not surprisingly, French is the official language of the French part of the island and Dutch is the official language of the Dutch part, however, English is commonly spoken throughout. Spanish and Papiamento, a local dialect that is a mix of Spanish, Portuguese, Dutch, and English, are also common. The literacy rate on the island is about 98%.

The standard of living on St. Martin is very good. Quality health care is accessible, the infrastructure is sound, and recreations abound. Beautiful beaches that offer year-round swimming and watersports, tennis, golf, gambling in exciting casinos, an exhilarating nightlife, and outstanding restaurants make the island one of the great tourist sites of the Caribbean. Note that although the French and Dutch sections of the island offer many of the same activities, they also possess their own atmosphere. Sint Maarten, the Dutch part of the island, has a vibrant personality and is certainly more bustling than French St. Martin, which in comparison is more tranquil. The Dutch capital at Philipsburg is cosmopolitan; the French capital at Marigot is relaxed. Either part of the island, however, ranks among the best of the Caribbean and is a wonderful place to visit or live.

St. Martin: Yesterday and Today

Columbus discovered St. Martin in 1493, but the island was not settled by Europeans until the 1630s when both the Dutch and French established outposts. By 1648, the two countries had peacefully divided the island and have maintained that peace right up into modern times.

The economy of the island has but one major sector: tourism. Indeed, the entire economy tends to revolve around the tourist trade, which is well supported by a solid infrastructure and quality ports and telecommunications system. The per capita income of the island is one of the best of the region.

The Benefits of St. Martin's Tax System

Unlike many islands of the Caribbean that offer a host of incentives to attract investment, St. Martin's principal benefit regarding taxes is its status as a free port. Unquestionably, it is one of the best in the world. No taxes or duties are required on items brought into the island or sent out. A wide assortment of products and items is available, with expensive jewelry, perfumes, electronics, and crystal being some of the most popular. Because of the free port status, savings on some purchases can be as high as 50%. Even on some of the most exclusive products, savings of up to 30% to 40% are not uncommon. Several Caribbean cruise lines include St. Martin as one of their scheduled stops just to allow their passengers the opportunity to shop.

If you would like to learn more about St. Martin, contact the following:

The St. Maarten Tourist Office
675 Third Ave., Suite 1806
New York, NY 10017
Tel: 212-953-2084 or 800 ST. MAARTEN
Fax: 212-953-2145

French Government Tourist Office
645 N. Michigan Ave., Suite 3360
Chicago, IL 60611
Tel: 312-751-7800

French Government Tourist Office
1981 Avenue McGill College, Suite 490
Montreal, Quebec H3A 2W9
Canada
Tel: 514-288-4264

French Government Tourist Office
30 St. Patrick St., Suite 700
Toronto, Ontario M5T 3A3
Canada
Tel: 416-593-6427

St. Maarten Tourist Bureau
Walter Nisbeth Rd., 23
Philipsburg, St. Maarten
Netherlands Antilles
Tel: 011-5995-22337
Fax: 011-5995-22734

Seychelles

Northeast of Madagascar in the Indian Ocean lies the archipelago of Seychelles. Although relatively unknown to most Westerners, Seychelles is gaining the attention of international investors because of programs that strongly encourage investment through various tax and business incentives.

Seychelles may be divided into two island groups. The Mahe group in the north includes the principal island, Mahe, and the nation's other most important islands. The second group is the small and uninhabited coral islands that extend southward. Although together the groups consist of some 118 islands, their total area is only 108 square miles (about 280 square kilometers).

Seychelles possesses a tropical marine climate highlighted by monsoon seasons. March to May, during the northwest monsoon, is the warmer season while late May to September, during the southeast monsoon, is the cooler season. Average annual temperatures are quite pleasant, varying little from 75 degrees F (*24 degrees C*). Rainfall varies among the islands but overall is plentiful, averaging about 90 inches (233 centimeters) per year.

About 78,000 people reside in Seychelles, with most of the population tracing its ancestry to Asians, Africans, and Europeans. About 90% of the people are Roman Catholic, 8% are Anglican, and the rest belong to other churches. Official languages are English and French, however, many people speak Creole, a tongue that has evolved from the many languages that have been spoken on the islands.

The standard of living in Seychelles is somewhat uneven. While it is very good in and around Victoria, the capital, in less developed areas the quality of life is more typical of third world countries than advanced societies. The literacy rate throughout the islands, for example, is only 58%. Due to effective policies that have resulted in economic growth, conditions have been improving in recent years, and Seychelles is developing as a prime tourist spot in its part of the world. Recreational activities include diving, sailing, and fishing, fine dining and entertainment in quality hotels, restaurants, and clubs, and the simple pleasure of enjoying one of the world's few remaining unspoiled natural settings.

Seychelles: Yesterday and Today

Although it is thought that Arab sailors visited the Seychelles as early as the 9th century, the islands of the archipelago were uninhabited when the Portuguese discovered them in 1502. The islands remained uninhabited until 1756 when the French claimed them, but it was not until 1770 that the French began to establish settlements. French authority did not last long, however. In 1811 the British gained control of the islands, and in 1903 the British made the islands a dependency of the Crown. Seychelles was granted independence in 1976. The country is a republic whose capital is located at Victoria.

Seychelles has experienced strong, relatively steady economic growth since the mid 1970s. During the last quarter century, per capita output has increased seven times over the prior levels, which were low by Western standards. The country's current per capita GDP is about U.S.$6,000.

For several years Seychelles experienced an average economic growth rate of 6% per year. The early nineties saw this rate slow, due primarily to the Gulf War conflict and an increase in public spending, however, by 1996-97, real GDP had rebounded to an average of 4.5%.

The strong economic growth has been a result of direct government initiatives that promote Seychelles as a financial and business center through supporting tourism, encouraging offshore banking, and developing freeport and export processing zones. The government has also taken steps to ensure that the infrastructure of the islands, which was well maintained by the British, continues to be one of the best of the countries in this area of the world. The telecommunications system is reliable, Port Victoria is the deepest port of the Indian Ocean and one of the most efficient of the region, and an international airport is able to manage the world's modern aircraft. These are major advantages, considering that Seychelles enjoys a strategic location in the paths of shipping lines and airlines.

In its continuing efforts to expand the nation's economy and raise the standard of living of its people, the government has enacted legislation that makes the trust laws and international trade zone laws of the Seychelles among the best anywhere. International trusts in Seychelles are not only easy to create, but quite valuable to investors who are seeking safety and privacy. It should be noted that the international trust is not available to residents of Seychelles, nor can a trust include any land in Seychelles. However, a Seychelles trust may own and trade in other shares, open and maintain bank accounts, or buy and sell government securities in the country.

The features of an international Seychelles trust include:

- The transfer or disposition by an individual who creates an international trust in Seychelles cannot be invalidated by any foreign rule of forced heirship.

- Settlors or trustees can also be the named beneficiaries of the trust.

- The settlor selects the law governing the trust, which is then considered to be the proper law.

- There are no restrictions on income from the assets of the trust.

- There is no requirement to provide the names of the settlor or the names of beneficiaries, unless a beneficiary is a Seychellois national or a body corporate resident in Seychelles.

- An international trust is valid and enforceable in Seychelles.

- It is not permitted to disclose or produce any information or document relating to an international trust, except under order of the Seychelles Supreme Court. Moreover, the purpose of any disclosure must focus on the trafficking of narcotics, dangerous drugs, the trafficking of arms, or money laundering.

  Thus, confidentiality is assured.

- An international trust may be established for a one-time fee of U.S.$100.

Since the early 1990s, much of the impetus of business laws has been to reduce controls on the economy while increasing liberalization.

The government's pro-business and pro-investment attitudes are the foundation of the country's economic success.

The Benefits of Seychelles's Tax System

Seychelles offers numerous tax incentives and other advantages to both individuals and companies. General tax incentives for investment include:

- No personal income tax.

- No withholding tax on dividends.

- No wealth tax, gift tax, property tax, capital gains tax, death duties, or taxes on properties.

Under the Investment Promotion Act (IPA) which was enacted in 1994 to encourage investment, specific tax incentives are available for both local and foreign businesses, including:

- Low business tax rate of 15% with further tax credits possible, resulting in a tax rate of 9%.

- In some cases, businesses may be eligible for a tax holiday.

- No import duties on capital equipment.

- An accelerated depreciation schedule of up to 150% of the original cost of assets for specific categories of investments.

- Under the International Trade Zone Act, companies that are eligible for an ITZ license are exempt from all taxes, provided their operations are aimed at an export market.

- 100% repatriation of capital and profits.

- Special incentives are available for investments in Export Oriented Units (EOU) and Special Growth Areas (SGA).

It should be noted that 100% foreign ownership is permitted in Seychelles.

If you would like to find out more about Seychelles, contact:

The Seychelles Embassy
820 Second Ave., Suite 900 F
New York, NY 10017
Tel: 212-972-1785
Fax: 212-972-1786

Seychelles Department of Tourism and Transport
Independence House
Victoria, Mahe
Seychelles
Tel: 248-225313, 224030
Fax: 248-224035, 225131

Ministry of Finance and Communications
Central Bank Building
P.O. Box 313
Victoria, Mahe
Seychelles
Tel: 248-382000
Fax: 248-225265

Development Bank of Seychelles
Independence Ave.
P.O. Box 217
Victoria, Mahe
Seychelles
Tel: 248-224471
Fax: 248-224274

Seychelles Chamber of Commerce and Industry
Ebrahim Building
P.O. Box 599
Victoria, Mahe
Seychelles
Tel: 248-323812
Fax: 248-321422

The Republic of Singapore

Positioned at the southern tip of the Malay Peninsula, at the crossroads of international trade routes and serving as a gateway to Asia, Singapore occupies an enviable site. This location, combined with the republic's pro-business climate, has resulted in one of the world's most robust economies. That the nation's government offers a host of tax incentives to encourage investment makes Singapore quite popular among international investors who seek ways to expand their businesses and reduce their tax loads.

Singapore is a tiny nation, its area of 224 square miles (580 square kilometers) being less than that of New York City. Comprised of more than 50 small islands, of which Singapore Island is the largest and on which the capital city of Singapore is located, the country rises little above sea level. Singapore's climate is tropical, typically warm and wet with an average annual temperature of 81 degrees F (*27 degrees C*) and an average annual rainfall of about 95 inches (240 centimeters). Although the wettest months are from November to January, there is little variation in temperature throughout the year.

About 3 million people live in Singapore. Chinese comprise about 77% of the population, followed by Malays, 15%, and Indians, 6%, however, drawn by Singapore's global economy, people from countless lands come to Singapore. Many languages are spoken, with Chinese, Malay, Tamil, and English being the most common. The language of government and much international business is English. Like the ethnic makeup of the population, various major religions are represented, including Buddhism, various Christian churches, Islam, Taoism, and Hinduism.

The standard of living in Singapore is one of the highest in Asia. Health care is of high quality, the literacy rate is 90%, and the country's infrastructure is excellent and undergoes constant modernization. Singapore has earned a reputation as one of the world's safest and cleanest cities that offers a modern cosmopolitan lifestyle in which boredom is rare.

Singapore: Yesterday and Today

In 1819 the Englishman Sir Thomas Stamford Raffles founded Singapore. Five years later, the Sultan of Jahore deeded the city to the British East India Company in perpetuity. In 1926 the city was incorporated into a colony of the Straits Settlement, remaining a British colony until 1959 when it became an autonomous member of the Commonwealth. Although Singapore became a part of the Federation of Malaysia in 1963, the federation lasted only two years, after which Singapore became a separate nation.

Singapore is a republic, based on a constitution of 1959. The country's government is modeled after the British system in which a prime minister is the head of government, but legislative power rests with a parliament.

Singapore's diversified economy is one of the strongest in Asia. Through much of the nineties, the nation's economy has expanded at a rate of 7% to 10%. Several sectors contribute to economic growth, including electronics, pharmaceuticals, chemicals, machinery, timber products, plastics, steel (particularly piping), rubber products, clothing, processed foods, shipbuilding, and oil refining. Global shipping services center around Singapore's deep water port, which is one of the best in the region and is the busiest port in the world in terms of shipping tonnage. International trade and the transshipment of products manufactured in Southeast Asia are cornerstones of the economy. The country has also become the major shipbuilding, ship-repair, and oil-rig construction center in this area of the world. Because of the capacity of its five oil refineries, it ranks as the third largest oil refining site in the world after Houston and Rotterdam.

In recent years, Singapore has also evolved into a financial and business center. Numerous international banks, insurance companies, traders, and financial services companies have established branch offices and subsidiaries in Singapore.

The nation's government is committed to free trade and its open economy provides opportunities absent in many parts of Asia. A variety of tax incentives and inducements make investment in Singapore quite attractive for many investors.

The Benefits of Singapore's Tax System

In an effort to encourage investment and maintain the nation's competitive edge over its rivals, Singapore's government offers several substantial tax incentives. While most of the incentives are aimed at businesses, individuals, particularly non-residents, may also benefit.

Following are tax benefits applicable to non-residents:

- Non-residents who remain in Singapore for not more than 60 days in a year are not subject to tax.

- Non-residents who remain in Singapore for more than 60 days, but less than 183 days in a year, are subject to tax on income from or received in Singapore at a rate applicable to Singapore residents or 15%, whichever is greater.

- Non-residents who remain in Singapore for more than 183 days in a year are considered residents and are taxed at a rate calculated on a sliding scale ranging from 2% on the first $5,000 to 28% on income greater than $400,000.

A variety of business tax incentives are available. Most of the incentives are offered under the Economic Expansion Incentives Act (EEIA) and administered by the Economic Development Board, the Trade Development Board, the Monetary Authority of Singapore, and the Ministry of Finance. The most significant tax incentives for businesses include:

- Pioneer enterprises are exempt from tax on qualifying income for a period of 5 to 10 years. The exemption may be extended, based on individual cases.

- A concessionary tax rate of not less than 10% on income that arises from qualifying activities for a period of up to 10 years.

- For companies engaging in business expansion, an exemption of corporate taxes for a period of up to 5 years on income that surpasses pre-expansion amounts.

- An exemption of corporate tax on 90% of qualifying export income for a period of 5 years, which, based upon individual circumstances, may be extended.

- An exemption of up to 50% of taxable income of an equal amount to a specified percentage of new fixed capital expenditure.

- A tax rate of 10% on income derived from approved services in Singapore for a period of up to 10 years. The time frame may be extended.

- A full or partial exemption of withholding tax on approved royalties.

- A full or partial exemption of withholding tax on interest payments.

- An exemption of corporate tax on 50% of qualifying export income in warehousing and servicing for a period of 5 years. The time frame may be extended.

- The qualifying income of an overseas enterprise is exempt from tax for a period of up to 10 years, provided the qualifying activity is deemed to promote the economic or technological development of Singapore. (Qualifying activities include such operations as manufacturing, services, infrastructure development and management, and tourism development and management.)

Specific tax incentives have been enacted that are designed to promote Singapore as a financial center. These include:

- Asian Currency Units and Approved Securities Companies are eligible for tax concessionary rates of 10% on income derived from various activities. (An Asian Currency Unit is a unit within a financial institution that has been approved by the Monetary Authority of Singapore to conduct its business in the Asian Dollar Market.)

- Income derived by a foreign investor from funds that are managed by an Asian Currency Unit is exempt from tax.

- Corporate members of the Singapore International Monetary Exchange are subject to a concessionary tax rate of 10% in regards to dealing profits, fees, and commissions.

- Income derived from an approved syndicated offshore creditor is exempt from tax under specific conditions.

Unquestionably, Singapore's impressive host of tax incentives can result in major tax savings for investors and companies. As an entryway to Asia, Singapore occupies a prime location. As a center for investment, it has few equals.

To learn more about Singapore, contact:

Consulate of the Republic of Singapore
231 East 51st St.
New York, NY 10022
Tel: 212-223-3331
Fax: 212-826-5028

Consulate of the Republic of Singapore
1670 Pine St.
San Francisco, CA 94109
Tel: 415-928-8508
Fax: 415-673-0883

The Singapore Economic Development Board
250 North Bridge Road, #24-00
Raffles City Tower
Singapore 0617
Tel: +65-336-2288
Fax: +65-339-6077

Tunisia

Tunisia lies on the coast of North Africa between Libya and Algeria. With an area of 63,170 square miles (163,610 square kilometers), the country is about the size of Georgia. Moving southward from the coast, low mountains descend to a central plain and finally give way to the Sahara Desert.

Not widely recognized as a site for investment, Tunisia in recent years has opened its economy and taken steps to attract investors, most notably by supporting a free-market economy and enacting legislation that offers various tax incentives. Tunisia's economy is quite diversified and its underlying strengths promise gains in the future.

Tunisia's climate varies with latitude. A temperate climate with hot, dry summers and mild, rainy winters is the norm in the north with dryer and eventually desert conditions prevailing in the south. Temperatures in the north average 79 degrees F (*26 degrees C*) in the summer and 51 degrees F (*11 degrees C*) in the winter. Moving southward, annual temperatures become higher. Although the overall country may be characterized as dry, annual rainfall in the north averages about 24 inches (61 centimeters) per year. The total, of course, is much less in the south. Indeed, in the far southern region of the country, areas may receive just a trace of rain in an entire year.

About 9 million people live in Tunisia. Some 98% are Arab-Berber with the rest of the population comprised of Europeans, Jews, and other minorities. Most of Tunisia's people are Muslim with 1% being Christian and another 1% Jews. The major language is Arabic, but French is also widely spoken. The literacy rate is close to 70%.

The standard of living in Tunisia is good in Tunis, the capital, and other major cities and towns, but declines in outlying areas, particularly in the south. Various recreational activities are available, including sailing, surfing, golf, tennis, riding, hiking, shopping and fine dining. In Tunis, professionals and the well educated enjoy the conveniences and lifestyle that may be found in any modern city.

Tunisia: Yesterday and Today

About 814 B.C. Phoenician traders founded the city of Carthage near the site of present-day Tunis. The city developed into a Mediterranean power and extended its authority over much of North Africa during the next several hundred years. After a series of wars with Rome, the Carthaginian Empire was destroyed in 146 B.C. and Tunisia became a part of the Roman Empire for roughly the next 600 years. After Rome fell, various people controlled Tunisia: the Germanic Vandals, Arabs, Spanish, and Turks. In 1881 the French seized control and made Tunisia a French protectorate, a tie that lasted until 1956 when France, acceding to the wishes of the Tunisian people, granted Tunisia independence. The next year, Tunisia redefined itself as a republic. Although the various people that held sway in Tunisia all left their legacies, French influence is the most profound and lasting.

Tunisia's republican form of government is based on a constitution adopted in 1959 and amended in 1988. The nation's laws have been developed from Islamic law and the French civil laws.

Tunisia's modern diversified economy is founded on agriculture, an expanding manufacturing sector, and growing tourism industry. Since the late 1980s Tunisia has achieved a growth rate of 5.4%, and in 1996 and 1997, real GDP growth was 6.9% and 5.6% respectively.

Foreign investors have clearly taken notice of Tunisia's economic success. Close to 20% of the private investment in Tunisia is from foreign sources, and more than 1,600 foreign firms or joint ventures are established in the country. Some of the most notable include: General Motors, Hoechst, Ericsson, Isuzu, Nabisco, Nestle, Northern Telecom, Philips, Pirelli, Shell, Whirlpool, Siemens, Sony, and Thomson. Total foreign investments are close to U.S.$4 billion.

Tunisia's infrastructure is one of the best on the continent and supports the nation's economic goals. The telecommunications system is efficient, and the country possesses several seaports and airports.

In its continuing efforts to promote the country's economy, the government encourages privatization and has taken steps to simplify the tax code. The government has also enacted legislation to stabilize the country's financial system, which is considered to be sound and effective in meeting the needs of investors and companies.

The Benefits of Tunisia's Tax System

Tunisia provides significant tax incentives for companies that operate in free trade zones. Generally, the incentives are available to both foreign and domestic firms.

- Companies operating in a free zone are exempt from taxes.

- Companies operating in a free zone are exempt from customs duties, except social security taxes for employees who decide to take part in the Tunisian social security system.

- Foreign investors may freely transfer their profits and any income that result from the transfer of assets.

Employees with non-resident status also benefit under the Tunisian tax code:

- Employees pay a flat income tax rate of 20%.

- Employees are exempt from customs duties and taxes on imports of personal goods. This includes one car per employee.

Should you wish to learn more about Tunisia, contact:

The Embassy of Tunisia
1515 Massachusetts Ave., NW
Washington, D.C. 20005
Tel: 202-862-1850

The U.S. Embassy in Tunisia
144 Avenue de la Liberte
1002 Tunis-Belvedere
Tunisia
Tel: +216-1-782-566
Fax: +216-1-789-719

The Tunisian National Tourism Office
1, Ave., Mohamed V
Tunis
Tunisia
Tel: +216-1-341-077
Fax: +216-1-350-997

The Tunisian Tourist Office
1253 McGill College
Bureau #655
Montreal
Quebec, Canada H3B 2Y5
Tel: 514-397-1182
Fax: 514-397-1647

The Republic of Turkey

As the bridge between Europe and Asia since ancient times, Turkey has enjoyed an enviable location. A crossroads of trade for centuries, its position has never been more important as the global economy expands and links between Europe, the Middle East and Far East become stronger than ever. Ready to take advantage of the country's prime location, the Turkish government has established free zones and tax incentives to attract investment, thereby building the nation's economy and improving its standard of living. For investors, Turkey offers excellent potential opportunities and significant tax benefits.

The country is large, about twice the size of California with an area of about 300,000 square miles (780,500 square kilometers), its land varying from mountains to broad fertile plains. The highest peak is Mount Ararat at 16,946 feet (5,165 meters), which the Bible records as the place Noah's Ark came to rest after the deluge.

Because of its vast area, Turkey has numerous climates, from long, hot summers along the Mediterranean and temperate zones in the central part of the country, to relatively short summers and severe winters in mountainous regions. Rainfall, which is abundant along the Mediterranean, gradually decreases as one moves northward.

Some 62 million people live in Turkey, about 80% of whom are ethnic Turks. The remainder of the population are Kurdish. The country's principal language is Turkish, with about 90% of the people able to converse with it; Kurdish and Arabic are also spoken. Close to 99% of the people are Sunnite Muslim. An important minority of Shiite Muslims live in the southeastern part of the country. Other religious groups, including Christians, comprise less than 1% of the population.

The standard of living in Turkey has improved steadily during the last twenty years. In the cities and major towns residents of an emerging middle class enjoy a modern lifestyle with access to quality health care, education, and recreational activities. The country's overall literacy rate is about 80%, up from 60% in the early 1980s.

Being a crossroads of east and west, Turkey has developed into a land of alluring history and culture. It is a distinctive land that offers numerous options and opportunities for investors.

Turkey: Yesterday and Today

Turkey has an ancient past and has been home to many people. Long before the Romans, major trade routes crossed the land. Once conquered by Rome, Turkey remained a part of the Empire for centuries and prospered from abundant commerce and trade. After the fall of Rome, Turkey was the center of the Byzantine Empire with its major city at Constantinople. The Byzantines carried on Roman civilization, albeit with strong Eastern influences, for the next thousand years. In 1453, the Ottoman Turks finally captured Constantinople and made it a part of a new empire that lasted for much of the next 400 years. Turkey finally became an independent republic in 1923. Much of the country's history throughout the 20th century has been beset by conflict from rival political groups. Since 1983, however, the country has been under civilian rule, a period which has seen widespread stability and economic growth.

This period of stability has enabled the government to concentrate on policies that foster economic growth, particularly industrial development. While agriculture has traditionally been the main sector of the country's economy, in the early 1990s industry surpassed agriculture in economic importance.

At the beginning of the 1980s, a major shift in economic policy led to a promotion of free market principles, a general liberalization of business regulations, and the encouragement of investment, particularly of foreign investors. The reforms led to significant stabilization of the economy and put in place the fundamentals for growth. Indeed, the nineties have been a time of generally steady growth with economic expansion averaging between 5% and 6%.

Perhaps one of the most important events of the eighties was the passage of the Free Zones Law (no. 3218) in June of 1985. Several free zones have since been created and are operational. All kinds of industrial activities are permitted at most of the free zones, with the exception of Istanbul Ataturk Airport and Trabzon Free Zones. Commercial and service activities including manufacturing, storage, packing, assembling and disassembling, trading, banking and insurance are some of the most common operations.

Turkey's overall infrastructure and telecommunications systems are good, particularly around the cities and major towns. Some outlying and remote areas, however, suffer from poor roads. In its efforts to promote the nation's economy, the government has invested heavily in a program of modernization.

The Benefits of Turkey's Tax System

Turkey offers a variety of important tax benefits to investors and businesses. Although Turkey does not provide many tax benefits to individual tax payers, it does offer advantages to non-residents.

- Non-residents who live six months or less in Turkey during the calendar year are subject to income tax only on income accrued in Turkey.

The major benefits bestowed by Turkey's tax code are associated with the nation's free zones. The country currently has six free zones in operation, with several more under construction. The following benefits are provided to companies operating within a free zone:

- A full exemption of income tax on income earned from activities in the zone.

- An exemption from corporate taxes.

- An exemption of value-added tax.

- An exemption from taxes for building and construction.

- An exemption from custom duties.

- A deferral for expenditures for research and development.

- Earnings from free zone activities may be transferred to any country, including Turkey, without restriction and free from any kinds of taxes, duties, or fees.

In addition, the following advantages are available to companies operating in Turkish free zones:

- Sales into the domestic market are permitted. This is seldom the case in free zones located in other nations.

- Infrastructure in the free zones is comparable to international standards.

- Bureaucracy is minimized.

- Access is efficient to major ports to facilitate shipping throughout the Mediterranean.

- Any currencies used in the free zone are convertible foreign currencies accepted by Turkey's Central Bank.

- Leasing arrangements are favorable.

- Access to skilled and unskilled labor is assured.

- Wages are relatively low.

Additional incentives are available to companies whose operations focus on export activities:

- An exemption from taxes, duties, and other charges.

- An exemption from value-added tax.

- Incentives for the use of energy.

- Exemptions from customs duties in regard to raw materials imported for export products.

- Special credits through the Export/Import Bank to foster exports.

- Credits for pre-shipment export.

- Credits for revolving exports.

Should you like to find out more about investment and tax incentives in Turkey, contact the following:

The American Turkish Council
1010 Vermont Ave., NW, Suite 1020
Washington, D.C. 2005-4902
Tel: 202-783-0483
Fax: 202-783-0511

The General Directorate of Foreign Investment
Inonu Bulvari 06510 Emek
Ankara
Turkey
Tel: 90-312-212-8914-5
Fax: 90-312-212-8916

General Directorate of Free Zones
Inonu Bulvari 06510 Emek
Ankara
Turkey
Tel: 90-312-212-5887
Fax: 90-312-212-8906

SIRTEC
555 Rene-Levesque Blvd. Est, 9th Floor
Montreal, Quebec H2Z 1B1
Canada
Tel: 514-866-1633
Fax: 514-875-5004

Turks and Caicos

The Turks and Caicos are two groups of islands that lie southeast of the Bahamas. The Turks are comprised of Grand Turk and Salt Cay, several uninhabited cays, and several tiny rocks and reefs. Six major islands comprise the Caicos group, with Grand Caicos being the biggest. The islands tend to be rather flat, arid, and stony. The area of all the islands combined is about 165 square miles (430 square kilometers).

The Turks and Caicos possess a tropical marine climate that tends to be dry with abundant sunshine, a uniformity brought about by the southwest trade winds. The average annual temperature is about 85 degrees F (29 degrees C), and rainfall is a meager 28 inches (70 centimeters) per year. Note, however, that hurricanes are a threat during the typical storm season from June to late October.

Of the Turks' and Caicos' 14,500 people, most are descended from Africans or are of mixed blood. Most of the people belong to Protestant churches with the Baptists, Methodists, and Anglicans having the most members. English is the official language of the islands, and the literacy rate is about 98%.

The standard of living on the islands is relatively good. Unlike many islands of the Caribbean that have purposely designed attractions to increase tourism, the Turks and Caicos are tranquil and offer a relaxed lifestyle. Of course, there is plenty to do on the islands, including dining at top restaurants, dancing in clubs, gambling in a casino, as well as enjoying water sports, golf, tennis, and shopping.

Turks and Caicos: Yesterday and Today

Before the arrival of the Europeans in the early 1500s, the Turks and Caicos were inhabited by native American Indians that likely migrated from the Orinoco region of South America. After the arrival of the Europeans the Indian population was destroyed through disease and enslavement within a generation, and the islands remained largely uninhabited until the 1670s when the Bermudans began to build the salt industry. British presence remained strong on the islands, and today the Turks and Caicos are a dependent territory of the United Kingdom. Much of the law of the islands is based on British laws.

Because of their dependency status, the islands have benefited from British support. This is most notable in their modern infrastructure and excellent telecommunications system. The islands are also economically and politically stable.

The economy of the Turks and Caicos is based primarily on tourism — about 50,000 people visit the islands each year — and offshore financial services. In an effort to support the financial services sector, the government of the islands has enacted legislation that encourages investment of virtually all sorts. Consider the following:

- Laws are conducive to conducting business in a tax- free environment.

- There are no exchange controls or restrictions on how much capital can be brought in or taken out of the country.

- Laws are favorable to the formation of offshore corporations, trusts, and financial services companies.

- The overall financial system is strong and is based on the U.S. dollar.

The Benefits of the Turks' and Caicos' Tax System

The Turks and Caicos offer some of the best and most significant tax incentives that may be found anywhere, including:

- No income tax.

- No tax on capital gains.

- No tax on corporate dividends.

- No tax on property.

- No withholding tax.

- No value added tax.

- No tax on estates, inheritance, succession, or gifts.

- No sales tax.

It is also noteworthy that the Turks and Caicos have not entered into tax treaties with any foreign government. Because there is no exchange of financial information with other agencies, privacy is enhanced. The island governments also maintain strict secrecy laws.

If you would like to learn more about the Turks and Caicos, contact:

Turks & Caicos Tourist Office
11645 Biscayne Boulevard, Suite 302
North Miami, FL 33181
Tel: 305-891-4117
Fax: 305-891-7096
Toll free: 1-800-241-0824

The United Kingdom

The United Kingdom consists of England, Scotland, Wales, and Northern Ireland. Often referred to simply as Great Britain, or England, the total area of the United Kingdom is 94,227 square miles (244,046 square kilometers) of land that is mostly low mountains, hills, and fertile plains.

Although Great Britain is rather high in the northern latitudes, the country's climate is tempered by the prevailing southwesterly winds of the North Atlantic, a current that is milder than much of the ocean over which it flows. The temperate climate of Great Britain, while often cool and somewhat damp, has few extremes in weather. Average annual temperatures range between 48 degrees F (*9 degrees C*) in the north and 52 degrees F (*11 degrees C*) in the south. Clouds are more common than sunshine throughout the United Kingdom, but overall rainfall is not extreme at an annual average of about 30 inches (76 centimeters).

The population of the United Kingdom is close to 60,000,000. People who consider themselves English are the dominant group, comprising about 80% of the population, with Scots, Irish, Welsh, Ulster, and other minority groups making up the rest. The Anglican Church has the greatest number of members, with Roman Catholics being the next largest religious group. Presbyterians, Methodists, Muslims, Sikhs, Hindus, and Jews are also represented in the population. The country's major language is English, though Scottish,

Welsh, and even some Gaelic are regional languages. The literacy rate of Great Britain is 99%.

The residents of Great Britain enjoy an excellent standard of living, on a par with other advanced countries. Health care is of high quality, and leisure activities are abundant and comparable to any western nation. Of course, the country's infrastructure is also of high quality.

Great Britain: Yesterday and Today

The history of England can be traced to as early as 3,000 B.C. when the island was inhabited by the Iberians, a people thought to be the builders of Stonehenge and other megaliths that dot the English countryside. Starting around 800 B.C. and continuing off and on for the next few hundred years, Celtic tribes from the continent made their way to the island and forced the original inhabitants to the north. One of these tribes was known as the Brythons and likely gave their name to the island, which became known as Britain.

In subsequent years, the Romans, various Germanic tribes — most notably the Anglos, Saxons, and Jutes — invaded the island and subjugated the now native Celts. For a time the Anglos were a dominant group and "Anglo-land" or "Land of the Anglos" likely gave rise to the name England.

The Germanic tribes dominated England for nearly 400 years until the Vikings began raiding the island's coasts. Eventually, some Vikings settled along the coasts and in time were absorbed by the population.

The last invasion of England occurred in 1066 when William, Duke of Normandy, known as the Conqueror, gained control of the country.

The Normans ruled England, however, in time, like the Viking invaders before them, they too were absorbed by the English population.

During the Middle Ages, England grew in strength, and by the Age of Exploration was one of the dominant powers in the world. It was during this time that English influence spread throughout the world via a colonial empire that was truly global in scope. Only after the two world wars was England eclipsed in world power by the United States. Nevertheless, Great Britain remains one of the world's major powers and its language, laws, and customs some of the most dominant throughout the world.

The United Kingdom today is one of the world's important economies, the fourth largest in Western Europe. Energy, an efficient financial services sector, and a strong agricultural sector are the foundations of the country's economy. An excellent infrastructure, highlighted by an advanced telecommunications system and numerous modern sea- and airports, support the economy. Note that the United Kingdom remains at the heart of the Commonwealth, a remnant from the era of colonization, but an organization that maintains significant economic muscle.

Throughout modern history, the financial system of Great Britain has been one of the world's strongest. This tradition continues. A good example of the sophistication of the financial services sector in Great Britain is Skye Fiduciary Services Limited, located on the Isle of Man. Directed by its chairman, Charles Cain, who is a former managing director of the second merchant bank to open on the island, Skye Fiduciary is one of the world's foremost offshore corporate and trust management companies. The firm offers a full range of company and trust management services and has exceptional experience in the creation of hybrid companies that function as a trust.

A hybrid company is an alternative to the traditional trust and is available in the Isle of Man. Hybrid companies serve specialized needs of wealthy investors, particularly in cases where a standard trust is too restrictive or is unavailable.

Hybrid trusts have their roots deep in British history. Because English law never provided for the formation of non-profit corporations, ordinary companies were formed with their owners agreeing to guarantee the debts incurred by the company, similar to the fashion U.S. shareholders guarantee the debts of a corporation to the limit of their individual stock investments. An important advantage offered to investors in a hybrid company is that the company can provide the same benefits as a traditional trust, though under a somewhat different structure.

Hybrid companies may be especially appealing to people who live in jurisdictions where conventional trusts are not recognized. Because hybrid companies can function as "quasi-trusts," their advantage to such individuals may be significant.

Skye Fiduciary Services Limited specializes in designing unique company structures to meet the needs of the international investor. Following is their address, phone, and fax numbers:

Skye Fiduciary Services Limited
 Attn: New Clients Dept.
 2 Water Street
 Ramsey, Isle of Man 1M8 1JP
 United Kingdom
 Tel: +44-1624-816117
 Fax: +44-1624-816645
 Direct communications to New Clients Information

The Benefits of Great Britain's Tax System

While there are not many incentives or benefits provided by the tax code of the United Kingdom, one provision can be quite useful. Prominent within the British tax code is the concept of "resident but not domiciled." Essentially this means that a person can reside, or live, in Great Britain but not be *domiciled* there, in other words, not maintain his or her permanent home in Great Britain. Under this definition, the individual may maintain his permanent home in another country.

There is a significant benefit to a potential taxpayer in this provision. An individual who is "resident but not domiciled" in Great Britain is required to pay taxes only on income that is actually brought into the United Kingdom. Such individuals can accumulate income that is earned abroad and not be required to pay taxes on this income in the United Kingdom.

Although entirely legal, the strategy is somewhat complicated and it is therefore vital to attempt to utilize it only upon the advice of a competent tax expert, one who understands British tax law. For some individuals, this provision can be quite valuable.

Should you wish to learn more about the United Kingdom, contact:

The British Tourist Authority
7th Floor
551 Fifth Ave.
New York, NY 10176
Tel: 212-986-2200

The British Tourist Board
40 West 57th St.
New York, NY 10019
Tel: 212-581-4700

The Embassy of Great Britain
3100 Massachusetts Ave., NW
Washington, D.C. 20008
Tel: 202-462-1340
Fax: 202-898-4255

The British Tourist Authority
Thames Tower, Black Rd., Hammersmith
London W6 9EL
England
United Kingdom
Tel: +44-181-846-9000
Fax: +44-181-846-9000

Uruguay

Uruguay is a rather large country of South America, bordered by Argentina to the west, Brazil to the north, and the Atlantic Ocean on the east and south. Its total area is about 68,037 square miles (176,220 square kilometers), spread over topography that includes low mountains, plains, plateaus, and coastal lowlands.

The country possesses a warm, temperate climate with average summer temperatures hovering around 71 degrees F (*22 degrees C*) and average winter temperatures at about 50 degrees F (*10 degrees C*). Temperatures generally don't fall below freezing anywhere in the country. Rainfall throughout Uruguay is moderate at about 35 inches (90 centimeters) per year.

Uruguay's population is about 3.2 million, with 88% of its people having descended from Europeans whose ancestors came mostly Spain and Italy. Mestizos, 8%, and blacks, 4%, comprise the rest of the population. About 66% of the people are Roman Catholic, 4% are Protestant, and 4% are Jewish; many Uruguayans don't formally practice any religion. Spanish is the dominant language, and 97% of the country is literate.

The standard of living in Uruguay is best around Montevideo, the capital, and other big cities where residents enjoy a lifestyle that rivals any in Latin America. Uruguayans have created a culture that celebrates art, literature, music, dance, and theater. Montevideo is a city of traditional colonial and modern architecture, featuring excellent restaurants, nightclubs, yacht and fishing clubs, golf courses, water sports, and casinos.

Uruguay: Yesterday and Today

Although the Spanish first explored Uruguay in the early 1500s, it was not until 1624 that they established the first permanent settlement on the Rio Negro. Throughout the colonial period Spain and Portugal contended for control of the region, with Spain winning out in 1777. Spanish authority was not long-lived, however. By 1814 Uruguayans expelled the Spanish governor, but Uruguay was quickly annexed by Brazil. Uruguayans regained independence in 1825, however, the road to stability was a long one filled with political turmoil and civil war. Indeed, the country suffered through internal conflicts into the 20th century.

Since the 1980s, Uruguay has achieved political and social stability. Under civilian rule, the nation has concentrated on building the economy and promoting the welfare of its citizens.

During the 1990s, the government has enacted legislation designed to open the country's markets, reduce inflation, and reform former stifling economic practices and regulations. Trade has been fostered through MERCOSUR (the Southern Cone Common Market).

Uruguay's economy centers around agriculture, meat processing, wine, leather goods, textiles, petroleum refining, and cement. While the infrastructure around Montevideo is adequate for most purposes, the country's telecommunications, air- and seaports, and road- and railways require modernization.

In an effort to bolster economic activity, the government has established various free zones, which can be privately or publicly held. There are few restrictions on the type of company or the operations of a company in the zones.

In January, 1998 a new law (Law 16.906) was passed to promote and protect investments. Applying to both foreign and domestic investors, the law guarantees equal treatment for all investors and simplifies the process for doing business in Uruguay.

The Benefits of Uruguay's Tax System

Compared to many countries, Uruguay has a rather complex tax system, however, free zones provide companies with excellent incentives, including:

- An exemption from all Uruguayan taxes, present and future for a minimum period of 25 years. (The only exception is the contribution to the state social security.)

Under the new investment law, the Executive Power may grant special incentives and benefits to companies or activities that are officially declared "promoted." The benefits include:

- An exemption from income tax, net worth tax, and and other taxes.

- An exemption from taxes on incorporation and taxes on the capital increases of the legal entity that is in charge.

- An exemption of up to 60% of the employer social security contributions applicable to the salaries of personnel.

- An exemption from tariffs and other charges on the importation of machinery and capital goods.

If you would like to learn more about Uruguay, contact:

The Uruguayan Embassy
1918 F St., NW
Washington, D.C. 20006
Tel: 202-331-1313 through 1316

Uruguayan Consulate
747 3rd Ave., 21st Floor
New York, NY 10017
Tel: 212-753-8581
Fax: 212-753-1603

Uruguayan Consulate
2715 M St., 3rd Floor, NW
Washington, D.C. 20007
Tel: 202-331-4219
Fax: 202-331-8142

Uruguayan Consulate
8000 Sears Tower Piso 78
Chicago, IL 60606
Tel: 312-876-8242
Fax: 312-876-7934

Uruguayan Consulate
1077 Ponce de Leon Blvd.
Coral Gables, FL 33134
Tel: 305-443-9764
Fax: 305-443-7802

Uruguayan Consulate
540 World Trade Center
2nd Canal St.
New Orleans, LA 70130
Tel: 504-525-8354
Fax: 504-524-8925

Uruguayan Consulate
429 Santa Monica Blvd., #400
Santa Monica, CA 90401
Tel: 310-394-5777
Fax: 310-394-5140

Tax Havens and Tourism

Tax havens are very much in the news, and stories about small- and medium-sized companies mushrooming overnight and multi-national giants amassing fabulous fortunes via tax haven operations are growing. They may sound like Alice in Wonderland fairy tales to most people, but to the sophisticated entrepreneur, use of foreign tax havens for such advantages is an everyday business opportunity.

The use of a foreign corporation domiciled in any one of the famous company tax havens such as Switzerland, Panama, the Bahamas, or Bermuda (among others, can enhance the profitability of any international business, and especially a travel or tourism enterprise.

Many European and American companies are expanding and diversifying overseas as a means of growth and as a hedge against economic ups and downs in their country of origin. By incorporating a tax haven operation to accumulate tax-free income, accomplishment of multi-national objectives is accelerated. A travel or freight operation can be established in a tax haven to be used as a conduit for international sales activity and financing. Such operations can accumulate trade discounts, commissions, advertising allowances, etc., completely tax-free while the parent or associated company can assume tax deductions by absorbing administrative and selling costs.

Before getting into the ways in which tax haven operations are used by various types of businesses, it is of eminent importance that the distinct difference is understood between two seemingly similar terms: "tax avoidance" and "tax evasion." Tax evasion has dubious and illegal overtones: for example, a company might falsify its financial statements so as to conceal its full liability to the tax authorities — that would be tax evasion — an infraction of the law and a very serious one.

Tax avoidance, on the other hand, is a legitimate method of minimizing or negating the tax factor. In simple terms, it is utilizing "loopholes" in tax laws and exploiting them within legal perimeters. This is the cornerstone of the tax haven concept.

Certain offshore companies can defer any tax until the profits are repatriated to the investor's home country. These are generally companies actively engaged in the conduct of a local business. In the travel business, such a definition is especially easy to meet. A retailer, or group of retailers, could set up their own travel wholesale operation in a convenient tax haven, such as Bermuda, and put all of their European business through it. The profits of the Bermuda firm would accumulate tax-free, and could be invested in other foreign operations.

In addition, a great many countries offer tax holidays of 5 to 20 years for new hotel construction, often including smaller hotels down to as few as ten rooms. A travel company or group of companies could easily invest some of their foreign profits in such a venture, continuing to build for tax-free profits. Among countries offering such incentives for hotel construction are Morocco, Jamaica, Tunisia, the Dominican Republic, Panama, most of the British-associated islands of the Caribbean, the French West Indies, and many, many more. Such concessions usually include an exemption from customs duties on building materials and fixtures.

Most developed countries do tax the current income of certain types of corporations controlled by their residents, such as leasing companies, and other financial enterprises dealing the parent company. But this concept of a controlled foreign corporation applies usually to passive or tax-haven type corporations, not to active businesses. But even for a passive business, a joint venture with foreign partners on a 50-50 basis will allow the income to accumulate tax-free since the company is not controlled by national of either country. If you are leasing aircraft, coaches, or whatever, consider a joint venture with your foreign partner whereby you set up a jointly owned company to receive some of the income. You will both profit by it, and have a tax-free pool of funds to invest together in other ventures. Such profits will not be taxed in the country of either partner until they are repatriated, since they are not controlled by either country's citizen.

Countries which have no income tax include Bermuda, the Bahamas, the Cayman Islands, Nevis, and the Turks & Caicos Islands. A number of countries do not tax foreign source income, including Panama and Hong Kong. Shannon International Airport in Ireland also has special concessions for service companies (such as travel operators) setting up in the airport area, but so far no travel company has taken advantage of these, although other service companies have.

The cruise ship operators have long been able to use Panama and Liberia, but they are about the only segment of the travel industry which has shown any understanding of the advantages of tax havens.

Many businessmen looking for tax haven opportunities would envy the daily opportunities open to the travel industry, and yet the travel industry rarely uses these opportunities — or even understands them. 100% tax-free dollars will grow a whole lot faster than 50% after-tax dollars.

Why Your Investments Also Need To Reside In A Haven

Once you are living a international lifestyle, or living in a residence haven, if not before, it helps to find a haven for your personal investments — bank accounts, mutual funds, unit trusts, annuities, etc. There are great advantages in creating a personal or family trust in an offshore tax haven or money management center. Having all of ones finances managed by professional offshore managers provides a great deal of privacy, and the ability to have somebody qualified and able to act on your behalf immediately in case of an emergency. And it is useful to put your money management on autopilot and concentrate on doing the things that you want to do, not to mention that 99% of the time professional fund managers will do a better job than you can. Another reason is that the your assets can pass privately to his heirs without the interference of government probate systems, or forced inheritance laws in the country where the bank accounts or investment portfolios are held. For Americans, offshore structures become particularly important for protection against lawsuits, and sometimes government forfeitures. Unfortunately, many other countries are following this American trend, so people from anywhere would do well to plan to have their offshore structures in place before there is a need. After all, you aren't disappointed if you buy fire insurance and your house doesn't burn down. Placing your investments in a proper structure plays the same role.

Tax havens truly become an important key for an investor who has any form of active business involvement — from something as limited as collecting copyright or patent royalties all the way up to a very active business. A tax haven company provides the permanent base that any company needs to deal with the world at large, since a company cannot effectively become portable and continue to do business. The tax haven company becomes the investor's interface between his personal lifestyle and the need to anchor the business somewhere and have it appear conventional to those it does business with.

The royalty earning investor may use a tax haven company to take advantage of treaties that eliminate the withholding taxes in the high-tax countries, and then the tax haven company can funnel the money tax free to the investor.

An investor with more active business involvements may use a company in a different type of tax haven — perhaps to publish a newsletter sold on a worldwide basis, or to own a fishing trawler working the high seas, or just as a place to register his personal yacht.

Solving The Worldwide Taxation Problem For American Citizens

American readers of offshore books are usually faced with the frustrating fact that much of what is said does not apply to them, because the U.S. taxes its citizens on a worldwide basis regardless of where they reside. Much of this problem can be solved with combinations of trusts and corporations, of the type of tax planning that The Harris Organization does for its clients (see the sections on forming trusts and corporations for more details). But this still leaves the American taxpayer struggling through the various hoops of the tax code to protect his wealth from taxation.

Many publications talk about the value of offshore techniques to defer taxes. Creation of an offshore business by an American citizen will generally defer taxation until dividends are paid, allowing untaxed profits to compound in the foreign corporation.

This "option strategy" also works for inheritance taxes. With proper tax planning, one can create a large estate, and if one renounces U.S. citizenship before death, that entire estate can pass tax free to ones heirs. Thus a person is able to maintain and use their U.S. citizenship for a lifetime, and then take the option of renunciation of citizenship when it is no longer relevant — perhaps when living in an overseas retirement haven. All of the residential tax havens just discussed become very suitable for an American pursuing this strategy.

The same strategy is effective for a non-U.S. citizen who has been a U.S. permanent resident for a number of years and then leaves the U.S.

This allows a person to work in the U.S. and accumulate wealth, while their accumulated savings out of the U.S. tax free when they cease being resident.

Sources of Help for Offshore Investing

There seems to be a tendency in some circles to look for offshore financial institutions that will deal anonymously, or let you use a false name. But do you really want to entrust your funds to an institution that doesn't care who it does business with? A bank that will give its Visa card to Mr. Anonymous? That's not a very safe depository, is it? None of the institutions on my recommended list will deal that way. They will want, and will check, references, and they want to deal only with persons of substance.

Britannia Corporate Management Limited

Another business specializing in the formation of offshore corporations and trusts is Britannia Corporate Management Limited, located in the Cayman Islands. Its president, Gary F. Oakley, is a Canadian with over 18 years of Cayman Islands residency. Britannia is licensed to manage investment holding and trading companies, real estate holding companies, patent holding companies, and insurance holding companies. It is licensed to incorporate and manage corporations registered in the Cayman Islands. As such, the firm can service as the registered office of a corporation, provide its secretary, officers and directors, or undertake any day-to-day functions that may be required. More information can be obtained by writing the following:

Britannia Corporate Management Limited
Attn: New Clients Information
P. O. Box 1968
Whitewall Estates, Grand Cayman
Cayman Islands
Britannia can be reached by fax at +1 345 949 0716, directing
your communication to New Clients Information.

Lines Overseas Management Services

For asset management and securities brokerage, Lines Overseas Management Services is one of the most respected businesses operating today. Notable is its independence from onshore influences. It does not have a parent company controlling it from a big country, and does not maintain subsidiaries. Lines Overseas Management clears its trades locally, leaving no paper trail on its client activities in New York, London, or elsewhere.

Rates on certificates of deposit and liquid accounts offered through Lines are generally higher than those available in other markets. The firm offers proprietary Visa Gold debit cards to access cash on deposit. Offshore asset managers are appointed to provide personalized service in the selection of investments in order to best meet specific client needs. These managers fully understand the investment and tax avoidance objectives of overseas customers.

Lines is clearly not for everyone, however. It only accepts accounts with US $250,000 minimums. One of its offshore asset managers has been widely recognized in best-selling books and periodicals. He is Scott Oliver, a British subject, who earlier helped to develop sophisticated trading systems for some of Wall Street's largest investment banks. Today, many

American estate planning attorneys refer their wealthiest clients to Oliver for financial advice. He has broad familiarity and expertise not only with publicly-traded issues of all kinds, but has a strong track record in private placements.

For more information, contact the following:

Mr. Scott Oliver
Offshore Asset Manager
Lines Overseas Management (Cayman) Ltd.
P.O. Box 1159GT, Genesis Building
Grand Cayman, Cayman Islands
Mr. Oliver can be reached by telephone at +1 345 949-5808
or by fax at +1 345 949-1338.

Skye Fiduciary Services Limited

Skye Fiduciary Services Limited are among the foremost experts in offshore planning. Under the direction of its chairman Charles Cain, formerly managing director of the second merchant bank to open in the Isle of Man, Skye Fiduciary is the most experienced offshore corporate and trust management business in the jurisdiction. Although Skye offers a full range of company and trust management services, their expertise in designing novel company structures to meet the needs of foreign clients is unique.

For further information, write the following:

Skye Fiduciary Services Limited
Attn: New Clients Department
2 Water Street
Ramsey, Isle of Man 1M8 1JP
United Kingdom
Their telephone number is +44 1624 816117. Fax service is available at +44 1624 816645; direct communications to New Clients Information.

JML Swiss Investment Counsellors

One of the leaders in Swiss financial management is JML Swiss Investment Counsellors, a firm which offers a unique style of financial management. Clients can customize and control their own portfolios and still receive comprehensive management advice from some of the world's best experts on financial matters.

Recognizing that investors have differing goals, time frames, and tolerance for risk, JML's managers work with their individual clients to help them target their unique objectives. This naturally requires continued surveillance and analysis of worldwide economic trends, political events, financial markets, currencies, and other factors which could make some investments particularly attractive and others most unfavorable. Few individuals have the time or expertise to undertake this kind of evaluation themselves.

Further information about JML can be obtained by writing the following:

JML Jurg M. Lattmann AG
Swiss Investment Counsellors
Germaniastrasse 55, Department 212
CH-8033 Zurich, Switzerland
Their telephone number is (41) 41 368 8233 and their fax
number is (41) 41 368 8299, Attention Department 212.

Weber Hartmann Vrijhof & Partners

Potential investors may also want to consider the expertise of Weber Hartmann Vrijhof & Partners, another independent Swiss portfolio management firm. The principals of this partnership, former bankers and portfolio managers, provide services to individuals, offshore trusts, and corporations in need of investment advice.

The minimum opening portfolio to be managed by this firm is $200,000 or equivalent. The management team here normally recommends that a portion of the portfolio be invested in hard currencies other than the U.S. dollar including the Swiss franc, French franc, German mark, and Dutch guilder. Respected for their conservative approach to portfolio management, the partners have recently invested heavily in short-term bonds and have achieved double-digit yields for their clients in 1995 and 1996.

For more information, you can write to the following:

Weber Hartmann Vrijhof & Partners Ltd.
Attn. New Clients Department
Zurichstrasse 110b
CH-8134 Adliswil
Switzerland
Their telephone number is (41-1) 709-11-15 and their fax
number (41-1) 709-11-13, Attention New Clients Department.

Dunn & Hargitt International Group

Recently, many international investors have become dissatisfied with the small annual return on Euro-dollar deposits.

This is why private and institutional investors throughout the world are looking at other areas where returns can be in the area of 20-25% a year, to help offset the high annual rates of inflation on luxury goods.

The Dunn & Hargitt International Group, founded in 1961, has specialized in doing research for developing Portfolio Management Programs that have the potential of providing investors with a high return on their capital by investing in a diversified portfolio trading in the commodity, currency, precious metals, and financial futures markets in the United States and throughout the world.

The Dunn & Hargitt group offers investors the possibilitiy of participating in several of the different pools that are managed by them by investing through the investment programs that are offered by their affiliate, Winchester Life in Gibraltar, but which are actually managed by The Dunn & Hargitt International Group.

At the time of publication they are offering three possible investment alternatives, including The Winchester Life Umbrella Account (which allows 100% of a client's money to be invested in a diversified futures portfolio), The Winchester Life 100% Guaranteed Investment Account (in which Lloyds Bank acts as custodian trustee and US Government Zero Coupon Treasury Bonds are set aside to guarantee the client's capital), and The Winchester Life 150% Guaranteed Investment Account (which is a similar program, but guaranteeing that the client will receive at least 150% of the value deposited with a maturity date at least ten years in the future).

The average net return for the 150% Guaranteed Investment Account over the last six years would have been 22% a year. The average net return on the 100% Guaranteed Investment Account over the last six years would have been 27% a year. The average annual net return for The Winchester Life Umbrella Account over the last twelve years would have been 35% a year.

The minimum accounts accepted are $20,000 for The Winchester Life Umbrella Account, $20,000 for The Winchester Life 100% Guaranteed Account, and $50,000 for The Winchester Life 150% Guaranteed Account.

Although commodities are a speculative form of investment, investors everywhere are diversifying part of their portfolios to take part in the considerable potential profit opportunities that are available in the commodity, currency, precious metals and financial futures markets. The programs devised by the Dunn & Hargitt International Group will make profits if significant trends develop in either direction; i.e. up or down. This does not mean that short term results are always profitable, however the Dunn & Hargitt proven trading systems can provide above average returns over the longer term. Their objective is to make a profit for their clients of between 20% and 40% per annum and their computer trading systems are geared to this level of performance.

For more information, contact:

The Dunn & Hargitt International Group
P.O. Box 3186
Department S-697
Road Town, Tortola
British Virgin Islands

The structure of the Dunn & Hargitt Group has been established so that no taxes are withheld from the client's investment on the international commodity, currency, precious metals and financial futures markets. Because of this they can only manage money for investors who are neither citizens nor residents of the United States.

The Dunn & Hargitt International Group offers complete confidentiality to all of its clients, and will not reveal any information on a client or on its accounts to any third parties.

Tax-Free Investing in the United States

Few Americans realize this, but the United States is considered a tax haven by many foreign investors. While U.S. citizens are struggling with federal, state, and local tax burdens of 40% or more of their total income, foreign investors often can invest in the United States tax-free or almost tax-free.

The country is not a straightforward no-tax haven like the Cayman Islands or the Bahamas. Instead, it has some complicated tax laws and tax treaties that, when taken together and fully understood, provide opportunities for the foreign investor to make low-tax gains in U.S. investments.

The United States encourages tax-free foreign investment because it needs foreign capital to finance the economy and the government budget deficit. For example, Congress generally imposes a 30% withholding tax on all interest payments to foreign residents and corporations. Foreign investors let it be known quickly that they would take their money elsewhere if the withholding tax remained, however, and exceptions to the tax now exist.

The great benefit of the U.S. tax haven for many foreigners occurs when the U.S. tax rules are combined with those of other countries. The United States taxes its citizens and residents on their worldwide income. But noncitizens and nonresidents are not taxed on income from certain sources within this country. As a result, there are a number of foreign individuals who invest in the U.S. in order to take advantage of these non-taxable situations.

As a nonresident alien, you can get these benefits in many situations:

- No U.S. taxes on bank-deposit interest

- No U.S. tax on capital gains earned on U.S. stocks and bonds.

There will, however, be some tax on dividends from U.S. stocks.

In cases in which a tax might be incurred, such as on dividends, this often can be reduced or avoided by locating an offshore corporation in a country that has a favorable tax treaty with the United States. The Treasury Department has renegotiated a number of the tax treaties, but there still are some under which the U.S. withholding tax rate on dividends is significantly reduced.

Investing in U.S. real estate used to be an easy way to tax-free income and gains for nonresident aliens. But the rules were changed in 1980, and the profits no longer will be tax-free.

American Options Investing

Since capital gains are generally not taxable to foreigners, obviously any investing program which makes its profits in the form of capital gains, rather than dividends, interest or other types of earnings, is highly desirable. Unfortunately, there are not many such investing programs.

But one that does exist is trading options on stocks or on a stock index (such as the Standard & Poor's 500 Index). Since the gain or loss from trading in options is a capital gain, any profits made by a foreigner from trading in such options are free from any tax imposed by the United States.

As many investors already know, options are notoriously speculative and most people who try trading in them wind up losing money. Therefore, in order to take advantage of this tax benefit, it is first imperative to find a method of trading options which has a good probability of actually making money.

Almost any method of trading options which has the chance of making an above average return also carries a commensurate high degree of risk. But some practitioners of the arcane art of options trading do manage to do better than others over the years. One such person who has done very well for his clients is Max G. Ansbacher, Chairman of Ansbacher Investment Management, Inc., located in the prestigious Rockefeller Center complex in New York City.

Mr. Ansbacher has a long and distinguished involvement with options. In fact, he is the author of the first book published on the modern form of options, titled *The New Options Market, Revised and Enlarged Edition*. It was originally written in 1975 and Mr. Ansbacher has been trading options professionally ever since. In addition to this book, which has become one of the all time best selling books on options, he has written two other books on investing, has lectured on options at over 50 investment conferences in both the U.S. and overseas, and is the creator of The Ansbacher Index which is broadcast over the world wide facilities of the CNBC cable network.

He manages accounts for investors in both the U.S. and overseas. What sets Mr. Ansbacher apart from many others is that he has an excellent record of bringing in above average profits for his clients. Since most people who buy options seem to lose money, we asked Mr. Ansbacher what the key was to his success. He replied, "Yes, I agree that most people who buy options do seem to lose money. But what many people don't realize is that the money which the options buyers lose, doesn't disappear from the face of the earth. Rather it becomes the profits of the options *sellers*. And therefore, I concentrate in *selling* options."

What Mr. Ansbacher was saying is that options trading is actually a zero sum game when one looks at the total overall economic effect. This means that buying and selling options in its total impact on the economy does not either create any money or lose any money (except transaction costs). If the sellers make money, the buyers lose money. And if the buyers make money, then the sellers must lose money.

Since the options *buyers* tend to be the ones who lose money, it therefore must be true that the options *sellers* are the ones who make money over the long run. We asked Mr. Ansbacher why this should be true. His answer was, "The options buyers tend to be less sophisticated than the sellers. They don't always carefully assess the chances that their stocks will really go up enough to make money when they buy a call. Similarly, if people think a stock or a stock market is going to go down, they often over estimate how much it is going to go down. They will buy a put which is going to lose money unless the stock makes a really unusually large move within a relatively short period of time. These are the options I sell."

Of course there is not an investment program yet invented which makes money on every single trade, and option selling is no exception. When we asked Mr. Ansbacher about this, he said, "Certainly there are times when we have losses, but we believe that the probability lies with the sellers. And so we usually find that every loss is matched by many more winners."

Selling options is something which has to be done very carefully, because the risk is high. We asked Mr. Ansbacher what he does to control this risk. He said that the first defense was to control the number of options which he sells. "I usually sell only about one fifth the number of options which margin rules permit me to do. The second line of defense is that I use stop loss orders, which in most instances will automatically get me out of the options before the losses rise to a point which I consider unacceptable."

He continued, "The most interesting line of defense and the most important from the point of view of making money, is that I sell out-of-the-money options. This means that I sell options which have a strike price which is a distance away from the current price of the underlying security." We should point out that a strike price is the level at which an option becomes effective.

What Mr. Ansbacher means is that if a stock is 100, for example, he will not sell the 100 strike price call, because it is too likely that the stock will go above 100 and he might lose money. Instead, he might sell the call with a strike price of 120. The stock would have to be above 120 at the option's expiration for the seller of the option to sustain a loss. Obviously it is less likely that a stock will go up 20 points than it will merely go up a few points. So, by selling out-of-the-money options, Mr. Ansbacher is able to shift the probabilities in his favor.

Another major decision which an options trader has to make is whether to be trading calls, which go up in price when a stock goes up, or puts which go up in price when the stock goes down. Mr. Ansbacher said that he makes this decision based upon a number of factors, including his long experience in the field. "One of the factors I rely upon, is my own Ansbacher Index. This Index tells me whether the puts or the calls are higher priced. Since I am selling these options, I will generally choose to sell the ones which are higher priced. I believe the Index also gives an indication of which way the stock market is likely to go in the intermediate future." Thus, Mr. Ansbacher can sell options on the stock market which will be profitable for his clients if the market moves as The Ansbacher Index indicates it is likely to do.

The minimum account which Mr. Ansbacher accepts is US$100,000, and he accepts accounts from people residing anywhere in the world.

Depending upon the type of account, the investor will receive monthly or quarterly statements giving the exact value of the account. Clients are encouraged to discuss their accounts personally with Mr. Ansbacher.

For more information contact:

Ansbacher Investment Management, Inc.
Attn: New Clients Information
45 Rockefeller Plaza, 20th Floor
New York NY 10111
telephone: (212) 332-3280
fax: (212) 332-3283; Attn: New Clients Information

Asset Allocation — The Key To Successful Investing

One of the newest forms of investments in America is called asset allocation. Basically what it means is that one investment is "allocated" to a number of different types of investments by a professional investment allocator. The reason for this allocation is that no one type of investment is the best in all investment climates, and no one type of investment is usually appropriate for all of one person's investment money.

By using an asset allocation program, a person can invest a large amount of his principal in one place, gaining ease of tracking the investment, while attaining the advantage of having a number of different investments to serve his different investment objectives.

The asset allocator performs the service for the investor of allocating varying amounts of a total investment into different areas of investing, such as income stocks, growth stocks, small capitalization stocks, etc., and a variety of fixed income securities.

For modest to medium-sized investments, one method of attaining even more diversification of investments, and expertise in the actual details of the investments, is to allocate the investment among various top-rated mutual funds. As is well known, mutual funds can perform a number of important tasks for the investor. Diversification among a large number of stocks is possible for even a relatively small sum of money. Expertise is available on any type of investment at a relatively low price. Last, there is great liquidity with ease of purchasing and selling.

The actual allocation into different mutual funds will depend upon three principal criteria:

(1) What is the risk to reward profile of the individual investor,

(2) What is the need of the investor for predictable current income as opposed to the desire for capital gains, and

(3) What is the state of the economic and investment cycles at the particular moment in time.

The first and most important criteria are clearly the needs of the investor. These outweigh any thoughts of where any market may be going or where an allocator believes that the most money can be made. The first need which needs to be addressed is the risk which the investor is prepared to accept. All investment involves some degree of risk, but that risk can rage from the minor risk of how inflation can impact an investment in the next 90 days, to the risk of a high flying initial public offering in a company which may have no earnings and no prospect for earnings in the foreseeable future.

The amount of risk which is appropriate for an individual investor depends upon both the investors actual economic situation and his psychological attitudes towards risk of loss. Human temperament plays a very large role in determining risk tolerance. For example, if a person remembers a period of his or her past where they did not have enough money to make ends meet, they may be very adverse to taking any risk at all. Their attitude may be, "We worked hard for that money, and we don't want to lose it."

Others may have almost the opposite approach. They may never have known deprivation, and may have earned a good income all their life. Their attitude may be that they can live very well on their current earnings, and so any savings can be used to speculate. If the speculation turns out to be successful, that will be great and they can raise their standard of living even further. But if the speculation doesn't work out, that's OK too because they will simply continue living as they have.

Thus a good investment allocator will first determine what the needs of his clients are with respect to risk. One method is to determine first how much money is needed to maintain the current standard of living of the investor, and if he or she is not yet retired, how much of the investment will be needed when they do retire. Whatever amount is needed for these purposes is then designated as income producing principal and is invested accordingly into low-risk, high-yielding investments.

The balance can then be invested according to the investor's wishes into areas which can offer the promise of large capital gains in the future. This is the risk portion of the principal, and care must be taken so that the allocator and the investor agree on what amount of risk is to be taken.

The third and equally important task of allocating is to attempt to maximize the return to the investor from the changes in the economic cycle. When business has been in a slump and starts to turn up with both interest rates and inflation low, the largest profits are typically made in the stock market. But as the economy continues to expand, interest rates will rise and so will inflation. These factors make the prognosis for the economy less rosy, and the stock market may start to gyrate, and then fall. Perhaps gently at first and then more rapidly. So the stock market is definitely not the place to be.

At the same time that the stock market is suffering from inflation, the price of hard assets such as gold, oil, and real estate could well be rising rapidly. It is in these areas that fortunes are made during inflationary periods in the economy.

And then as the economy finally begins to cool down due to the effect of high interest rates, interest rates will begin to fall nd the big money may be made by investing in long-term non-callable bonds.

Thus a good allocator must keep in mind the needs of the individual investor and the current status of the economy. And of course he must have an intimate familiarity with specific investments which are available to investors. Whether they be stocks, bonds, or fixed income securities, the allocator must know which are appropriate for the investor and which will likely do well in the present stage of the economy.

Our favorite allocator is Max G. Ansbacher, a man who has been a practicing lawyer and is still licensed to practice law. He has had over twenty years' experience with stocks and stock markets. He is the man we recommend for options in the section above, and his credentials in the stock market are equally impressive. The second book he wrote is titled *How to Profit from the*

Coming Bull Market and it was published in the summer of 1981 near the bottom of the long bear market which had actually begun in 1973.

This book explained how and why a strong bull market was about to start on Wall Street. At the time it was published the book was largely ignored by a public which had grown cynical about a stock market which seemed to do nothing but go sideways or down, year after year.

But just one year after Mr. Ansbacher's book was published, the market suddenly took off like a rocket in August 1982 to start one of its greatest bull markets ever, and to establish Mr. Ansbacher's reputation as an insightful student of the stock market. Today Mr. Ansbacher heads up his own firm, Ansbacher Investment Management, Inc., located in Rockefeller Center, New York City.

We recently asked Mr. Ansbacher what his philosophy was concerning asset allocation. He replied, "Asset allocation is probably the most important single aspect of any investment program. And yet what is so strange about it is that it is often not even considered by investors. Some people will have most of their money in the stock market most of the time, unaware of the large risks which the market sometimes contains. Others believe in bonds, and continue to invest most or all of their money there, apparently unaware that in the 1970's and early 1980's the bond market was the biggest money loser of any investment. I would say that asset allocation is not just important, it is the key to successful investing."

In view of the importance which asset allocation has, we wondered just how Mr. Ansbacher went about handling an asset allocation account for a client. "The first thing I do is to talk to the client in whatever depth is necessary to determine the proper risk profile for the client. This depends upon his current financial situation and what he foresees for his future situation as well as his psychological feelings towards money and the potential loss of money. The second thing I do is to make an outline of the client's need for current income. This naturally has a great deal of influence on how we can invest the funds."

"Only after this has been done, do I then discuss with the client where I think the financial markets are heading and where the best returns are likely to be made in the future. The first step in actually making the investments are to decide upon the proportion of money going into each class of investments. The second part is to select the actual investments. For a number of reasons, I select from among the thousands of mutual funds which are available in the U.S. They range all the way from bond to preferred stocks, to common stocks of all types. There is usually a time and a place for almost all of them, but we try to pick the best one for that particular client at that particular time in the client's life, and in the life of the markets."

Mr. Ansbacher explained that his minimum investment is $100,000, and that he works with some of the biggest mutual fund organizations in the U.S., including Fidelity, Dreyfus and other mutual fund management firms. He does not bill his clients for a fee or commission for the work he does, because his compensation is paid to him by the mutual funds.

We have always believed that to be a good asset allocator is one of the most difficult tasks in the investment world, because it requires so many different considerations. To see just what kind of factors Mr. Ansbacher considers we asked him how he would go about planning an asset allocation program for a client whom we made up.

We gave him as an example of a potential client, a 50-year-old German married man who earns the equivalent of $200,000 a year and has a well-funded pension plan with his company. He is in good health and plans to retire at about the age of 65. We asked Mr. Ansbacher to assume that this man comes to him with $300,000 to invest. Here is how Mr. Ansbacher went about making his asset allocation process.

Mr. Ansbacher thought out loud, "The first question I have is about the amount of $300,000. Since he has a pension plan with his company, it is obviously not pension money. It is also a rather large amount for a person earning $200,000 to want to invest in the U.S. Is it inherited money? Does his wife earn money? Is this his life savings? Did he make a successful investment? The reason I ask this question is that it is very important to know if the money is replaceable. If it is inherited, will there be more to follow, or is this all? First I would want to know whether there will be more money coming in or not."

"Second, I would want to know more about his potential future obligations. Do he or his wife having living parents or other relatives who may need financial support in the future? How much support, if any, does he expect that his children will need in the future? Does he have disability insurance or a company plan in case he becomes disabled before he retires? Is there some specific financial goal that he has, such as acquiring a vacation home, yacht or other item which will require a substantial amount of ready cash. All these factors related to the amount of risk which I would want to take."

"The next set of considerations center around his financial situation now. Since he lives in Germany, this means that he pays a high tax on income such as dividends and interest, but pays no capital gains tax. Right away that sways me into investments which are likely to have high capital gains. I would want to know whether the $200,000 he earns covers all of his current expenses, or whether his current standard of living is so high that he needs extra income each year."

"Once we have the answers to these questions, we can begin to solve the problem of how best to allocate this investment. If there are no likely financial needs coming up in the future, and if at the time of the investment I decide that the stock market is not over priced or likely to decline for other reasons, I would place most of the money into various stock funds. I am particularly fond of funds which use value investing, which means that they pick stocks based upon how large an amount of earnings one gets for each dollar invested. This is another way of saying that they seek out stocks with high quality and low price/earnings ratios."

"The reason I like value investing is that many studies have shown that low price/earnings stocks outperform other stocks in normal markets. And in down markets heir inherent value keeps them from falling as far as others. The second group of stocks I would pick would be senior growth stocks. This means stocks which grow year after year because they are gaining market share, or because they are in a solid growth industry. Examples of this are some pharmaceutical companies which are constantly creating new and better drugs, or highly efficient national retail chains which are constantly gaining market share over local competitors."

"One advantage which growth stocks have for this particular client is that they usually don't pay a very large dividend, which fits right in which his local tax structure. Depending upon the wishes of the client, we would consider some gold stocks as a hedge against inflation. And we might add some mutual funds which specialize in large capitalization companies, because these are the tried and proven winners among all the competition in the economy, and often outperform other stocks when the economy softens."

"I would also place a portion of the assets into a short or medium term bond fund for three reasons:

(1) This could be a source of money in case an emergency arose which required a withdrawal from the fund,

(2) It is a reserve in case some outstanding bargains come up for investment, and

(3) It is a hedge against a downturn in the stock market."

Of course the actual percentage allocations would be discussed with the client. The actual funds selected would depend upon their performance records at the time of the investment. And in general, much of the allocation would depend upon the state of the economy at the time of the investment."

We thanked Mr. Ansbacher for sharing his thoughts with us, and for giving us an inside look at how he goes about this critically important task. We believe that he is one of the very best people working with investors to achieve their personal financial goals, through custom tailoring an investment allocation to their personal needs. Investors interested in using his services can contact him as follows:

Ansbacher Investment Management, Inc.
Attn: New Clients Information
45 Rockefeller Plaza, 20th Floor
New York NY 10111
telephone: (212) 332-3280
fax: (212) 332-3283; Attn: New Clients Information

Tax Freedom: Some Final Thoughts

Taxes are a major concern for every serious investor. The math is easy. For every dollar paid to the government in taxes, one dollar less remains in the taxpayer's accounts. While government clearly needs revenue to function, not all methods of obtaining funds are equal.

Some jurisdictions prefer to collect virtually all of their revenues from the income of their citizens; others, because of specific conditions and factors, develop other means. Some places, perhaps because they are small and their need for revenue is limited, are able to maintain low tax rates. Others, because they are small and have various sources of income — perhaps a tax related to tourism — do not tax their own citizens at all. Yet others, because they are promoting free zones or investment, are willing to forego tax payments for certain operations through tax holidays, deductions, or outright exemptions.

The astute investor is painfully aware of the effect on taxes on his or her assets. Unfortunately, aside from IRAs, employee shielded investment plans, and some types of bonds (which usually pay a very low interest rate), there are few good plans that offer an acceptable return on your investment while minimizing tax consequences.

The knowledgeable investor, therefore, seeks jurisdictions that legally reduce his or her tax obligations. As described throughout this book, many such places exist. Through proper planning and investing, most investors can reduce their taxes. Some will be able to eliminate their tax exposure entirely. All owe it to themselves and their families to investigate tax-free jurisdictions.

About the Author

Adam Starchild is the author of over twenty books, and hundreds of magazine articles, primarily on business and finance. His articles have a appeared in a wide range of publications around the world — including *Business Credit, Euromoney, Finance, The Financial Planner, International Living, Offshore Financial Review, Reason, Tax Planning International, Trusts & Estates*, and many more.

His personal website on the Internet is at http://www.cyberhaven.com/starchild